RtI: The Forgotten Tier

A Practical Guide for Building a Data-Driven Tier 1 Instructional Process

Joanne Klepeis Allain

Nancy Chapel Eberhardt

D1288837

Rowe Publishing
and Design

1 3 5 7 9 8 6 4 2

Printed in the United States of America

Rowe Publishing
and Design

www.rowepublishingdesign.com

Stockton, Kansas

DEDICATION

This book is dedicated to Jeanne Klepeis Young,

who displays immense courage in the face of impossible challenges.

Being in her company makes us all better human beings.

She has been our inspiration.

ACKNOWLEDGMENTS

We want to thank the countless administrators and teachers who have informed the focus of this book. To a large extent, the content of *RtI: The Forgotten Tier* is in response to the myriad of questions—simple and complex—that we have been asked during our work in professional development and coaching support. The questions encouraged us to clarify the confusing, provide many concrete examples, and whenever possible support our words with graphics and tables. We also want to thank everyone who provided us with feedback during the development process. Our end result is infinitely better for the comments and queries along the way.

A special thanks goes to our editor, Lesley Quattrone. Her background in education, her grasp of our intent, and her talent with language merged our two writing voices into a single coherent text. We are deeply indebted to her for her contribution.

ABOUT THE AUTHORS

Joanne Allain, a national RtI consultant with 3t Literacy Group, works with states, districts, and schools across the country to develop, implement, and coach practical, customized RtI plans and instruction. Her career experience at both the classroom and district level provides the unique perspective of a practitioner in real schools with real children. As part of the planning process, Joanne focuses on the multiple roles educators play in increasing student achievement and providing the collaborative expertise needed for a comprehensive program.

She works closely with RtI teams, teachers, and administrators at primary, intermediate, middle, and high school levels. Joanne is the author of *Logistics of Literacy Intervention: A Planning Guide for Middle and High School* and *Logistics of Literacy Intervention: An RtI Planning Guide for Elementary Schools*.

Nancy Chapel Eberhardt currently works with districts and schools to implement RtI systems that focus on literacy instruction and intervention. Her career in education has included roles as a special education teacher, diagnostician, mainstreaming associate, and district-level administrator. In these various capacities, Nancy has done extensive teacher training, professional development, and diagnostic assessment.

Nancy has also worked as both editorial director and coauthor in the development of *LANGUAGE!* (Editions 2–4, a product of Cambium Learning Group), a comprehensive literacy curriculum for upper elementary, middle, and high school students with low literacy skills. Through this curriculum, Nancy's goal has been to translate literacy research into instructional practice to help all students learn to read, spell and write.

The authors are available for training and coaching support
to implement the process presented in this book.

Email us at:
Joanne.allain@3tliteracygroup.org
Nancy.eberhardt@3tliteracygroup.org

Or visit our website:
www.3tliteracygroup.org

CONTENTS

About this Book 1

Introduction: Tier 1—The Potential of RtI 3

Section 1: Foundations of Tier 1—Standards, Effective Practices and Data . . . 9

Chapter 1: Standards—The Foundation of a Successful Tier 1 Program 11
    The Case for Standards-Based Instruction 11
    Determining High Value Standards 12
    The Blueprint: A Logically Designed Scope and Sequence 13
    The Case for Curriculum 14
    Teaching the Standards to Meet the Needs of All Students 14
    Practical Application: Reflecting on the Standards 18

Chapter 2: The Case for Cognitive Preparation for Instruction 19
    Instructional Anticipation: The Starting Point 19
    The Task-to-Results Match 20
    Gradual Release of Responsibility—The Teacher to Student Transfer . . 22
    Grouping 23
    Engaging Students in Instruction 24
    Providing Feedback 25
    Threshold of Tier 1 25
    Practical Application: Inventory Your Strategies 26

Chapter 3: What's Data Got to Do With It? 27
    Using Data: From Global to Specific 27
    The Terminology Conundrum 28
    Focus on Purpose 29
    Tier-Specific Purposes for Data 31
    Different Decisions, Different Data 31
    Predictable Patterns of Assessment 32
    Managing the Data You Have 33
    Documentation 34
    Cut Points, Trend Lines, and Other Decision-Making Guidelines 35
    Now What? 40
    Practical Application: Inventory Your Assessment Tools 41

Section 2: Practical Application—From What to How. **43**

Chapter 4: Using Historical Data to Plan Initial Instruction 45
   Data Source: Historical Student Data 45
   How Does the Data Inform Instruction. 46
   National and State Test Data 46
   Classroom RtI Triangle. 47
   Use the Triangle for Instructional Planning 48
   Practical Application: Create Your Own Baseline Triangle 50
   Standards-Based Benchmarks 51
   Practical Application: Determining Patterns of Strengths
      and Weaknesses 53
   Screening Results. 54
   Practical Application: Determining Grouping Configurations and
      Related Needs for Supplementary Materials 55
   Demographics. 56
   Practical Application: Considering the Diverse Populations in
      Your Class 57
   Multiple Layers of Data 58
   Practical Application: What Does the Data Tell You? 60

Chapter 5: Before Instruction 63
   Let the Teaching Begin 63
   Data Source: Pre-Assessment 63
   How Do the Data Inform Instruction? 66
   Frontload Instruction 66
   Practical Application: To Frontload or Not to Frontload. 69
   Gradual Release of Responsibility 70
   Practical Application: Gradual Release of Responsibility 72

Chapter 6: During Instruction 73
   During Instruction: Responding to Student Performance 73
   Data Source: Formative Assessment 73
   How Do Formative Assessments Inform Instruction? 75
   Observational Data to Increase Engagement. 76
   Practical Application: Engage Students in Their Own Learning. 79
   Monitoring Student Work to Target Feedback 80
   Practical Application: Structuring Feedback 83
   Grouping to Re-Teach, Reinforce, and Enrich Based on CBA. 84
   Practical Application: Grouping Students Based on
      Formative Assessment. 86
   Beyond the Threshold of Tier 1? 87

Chapter 7: After Instruction 91
   Data Source: Summative Assessments 91
   How Do the Data Inform Instruction? 92
   Revise Your RtI Triangle 93
   Practical Application: Reconfigure Your Class Triangle 95
   Use Summative Data to Reflect and Move Forward 96
   Practical Application: Reflect and Look Forward 97
   The Cycle of Assessment and Instruction 98

Section 3: Considerations Beyond the Tier 1 Classroom **99**

    Chapter 8: Tier 1 Considerations Beyond the Classroom Level 101
        Implications of Tier Proportions 101
        The Changing Demands K–12 102
        An Unintended Downside of Tier-Specific Programs: From the
            Student's Perspective 104
        The Threshold of Tier 1: When the Gap is Too Great—Core
            Replacement 105
        Supporting and Sustaining a Tier 1 Initiative. 106

    Chapter 9: Start Where You Are! 107
        Tier 1 Checklist. 108
        District and School Examples 110

References 119

ABOUT THIS BOOK

RtI: The Forgotten Tier is designed for teachers and administrators grappling with the development and implementation of Response to Instruction and Intervention, more commonly referred to as RtI. In our effort to translate the intent of RtI into practice, our observations and experiences with hundreds of educators have led us to focus on Tier 1. Even though what to use, when to use it, and how to access intervention in Tiers 2 and 3 are essential questions in an RtI model, we focus on the Tier 1 classroom as the foundation of a successful RtI implementation. Our purpose is to provide a blueprint for the kind of instructional planning and decision-making that maximizes learning for all students—those who are proficient and advanced, as well as those who require intervention services. Making an investment in effective instruction for Tier 1 classrooms reduces expenditures by minimizing referrals for more intensive and expensive instructional support. A strong Tier 1 is cost effective for everyone—administrators, teachers, and students.

The chapters that follow guide you through a process designed to zero in on critical aspects of Tier 1 instruction—those aspects that when addressed contribute to teacher success and student achievement. Section 1 focuses on several critical instructional variables—what to teach, how to teach, and how to determine what students have learned. Section 2 takes the next step and demonstrates how these variables play out in effective Tier 1 instruction. Using data to guide instructional decisions and assess student progress are at the heart of building a strong foundational program. Section 3 examines decisions that exist beyond the Tier 1 classroom. These decisions pertain to infrastructure, policies, and overarching instructional goals that typically lie within the purview of school or district-wide leadership. This section also summarizes the process, presented as a checklist, designed to help you determine the state of Tier 1 in your classroom, school, or district. We invite you to take a look at the checklist in Chapter 9 as a pre-organizer for where you are in this process. We hope these chapters will foster conversation about the importance and effectiveness of first instruction. When educators actively address these issues, the critical role of Tier 1 will not be forgotten; it will rise to the forefront.

Joanne Klepeis Allain

Nancy Chapel Eberhardt

Tier 1—The Potential of RtI

What is RtI?

Response to Instruction and Intervention[1], commonly called in educational jargon RtI, was formulated during the re-authorization of Individuals with Disabilities Education Act (IDEA) in 2004. RtI promotes a multi-tiered system focused on providing students with increasing levels of instructional support, usually represented by three tiers. That system is the mechanism through which the core curriculum (Tier 1) is taught to students with the expectation that those with more intense needs will receive increasing levels of intervention (Tier 2 or Tier 3) in addition to grade level instruction. RtI encourages educators to draw upon the extensive body of research from across a variety of fields to do what is best for all students. In contrast to the "silo" approach of population-specific programming (Special Education, English Language Learner, gifted, general education), the multi-tiered model places the emphasis on students' needs, not labels. Such an approach has instructional benefits for students, cost benefits for schools, and frees up districts to look at needs and allocate resources accordingly.

RtI and Tier Proportions

One tenet of an RtI system is that resources are allocated according to student need. In a multi-tiered model, resources are in theory allocated based on the proportion of students requiring those services. Although services are provided along a continuum based on student need, the ideal configuration is represented by 80% of students requiring only Tier 1 services, 15% of students requiring additional Tier 2 services, and approximately 5% of students requiring the most intense services in Tier 3 (Batsche, et al 2006). This graphic depicts the ideal configuration. The darker the shading, the more resources are allocated to meet students' needs.

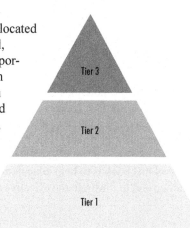

---

[1] For more information about RtI, we recommend the following websites:
RtI Action Network: www.rtinetwork.org; Center on Instruction: www.centeroninstruction.org

The proportion of students requiring services in each tier demands that educators examine current instructional practice according to those proportions. To reach the eighty percent goal for Tier 1, educators have generally and understandably taken the tack of devoting significant energy and personnel to Tier 2 and Tier 3 interventions in an attempt to boost more students into Tier 1. However, with the spotlight on methods and materials for Tiers 2 and 3, Tier 1 has become the forgotten tier. The goal of having 80% of students achieve Tier 1 status does not begin and end with developing Tier 2 and Tier 3 interventions. The key to unlocking the potential of RtI lies in creating strong and effective good first instruction in Tier 1.

Knowing how close a school is to the ideal proportion impacts the focus of instructional analysis and decision-making as well as resource allocation. If the percentage is lower than the goal, then improving Tier 1 is of primary importance. If the percentage is on or close to the target, educators can devote attention to other instructional considerations. Whether a school or district is new to or experienced in the RtI process, Tier 1 requires careful planning and attention to meet the needs of students. Indeed, the proportion of students in each tier is a strong indicator of the impact of previous school improvement efforts and the effectiveness of the current system. Strengthening Tier 1 instruction helps guarantee fewer students will require Tier 2 or Tier 3 intervention, thus helping to achieve the goal of 80% of students performing at grade level. We will take a closer look at this in Chapters 5 and 9.

When planning effective Tier 1 instruction, it is important not to lose sight of students who are proficient and advanced, while addressing the needs of those who are struggling. RtI is not simply about providing never-ending intervention. It is about strengthening the entire instructional system so that as many students as possible are successful in Tier 1.

RtI Goes Both Ways

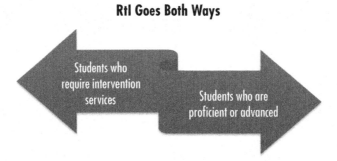

To realize the potential of an effective multi-tiered model, educators need a clear picture of what the Tier 1 classroom should look like, as well as the teacher's role in that classroom. Tier 1 is intended, after all, as the foundation upon which all supplementary interventions are constructed. It is the context in which teachers differentiate instruction to promote proficiency in most students, while reducing students' lack of engagement. The purpose of this book is to help educators identify essential components of successful Tier 1 instruction and to illustrate the effective use of data to get there.

Tier 1 Instruction Defined

Before we can draw a detailed picture of Tier 1 instruction, we need to define what we are looking for. A review of the RtI literature suggests that Tier 1 instruction:

- focuses on standards woven into a core curriculum;
- differentiates instruction for learners; and
- employs a monitoring and assessment system that identifies students who need intensive assistance beyond the general education classroom.

The working definition for the purposes of this book is as follows:

> *Tier 1 instruction is the practice of meeting the needs of the **entire range of learners** in a classroom by teaching a **standards-based core curriculum**, using multiple delivery models and research-based instructional strategies and materials. A variety of instruments serves to monitor students' progress and gauge their achievement. Tier 1 instruction is the **threshold for response to instruction** prior to the provision of more time or instructional intensity (i.e., movement to Tiers 2 or 3 for intervention).*

This definition combines the necessary components and approaches to Tier 1 instruction in a classroom of diverse learners. It mandates that teachers not simply deliver instruction; they also ensure that children learn. Our definition recognizes that Tier 1 has limits; students who fail to respond to Tier 1 differentiation (as evidenced by data gathering) may receive Tier 2 or Tier 3 services. The role of the Tier 1 teacher is to deliver a standards-driven, researched-based curriculum to all students. Teachers employ a variety of instructional strategies based on best practices and the needs of the learners, as well as gather data to monitor learning and assess student achievement.

How to Get There

The definition of Tier 1 is the starting point for creating a clear picture of a strong and effective Tier 1 classroom and role of the Tier 1 teacher. Much has been written about RtI in the primary grades. In contrast, this book focuses on what Tier 1 looks like in the context of a multi-tiered system beyond the primary grades. In upper elementary, middle, and high school, this often means that teachers are responsible for multiple classes of students in their subject area, making nearly any change in the process more challenging. While we acknowledge this reality, as students get older, their needs don't diminish or disappear. For this reason, we advocate that the ideas and process in this book need to be taken to scale at all grade levels.

We have structured *RtI: The Forgotten Tier* in three sections that offer a step-by-step process for analyzing and improving Tier 1 in your classroom, school, or district.

Section 1: Foundations of Tier 1—Standards, Effective Practices, and Data

This section focuses on several critical instructional variables—what to teach, how to teach, and how to determine what students have learned. Since English/Language Arts is foundational to all subjects, most of the examples and illustrations will focus on reading, writing, speaking and listening. The chapters in this section map out the relationship between these three key variables.

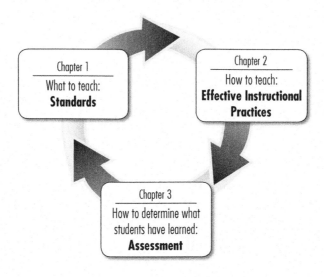

Section 2: Practical Applications—From What to How

This section takes the next step, the practical application of these essential variables to guide instructional decision-making and to determine progress. The chapters in this section focus on four distinct stages in the process.

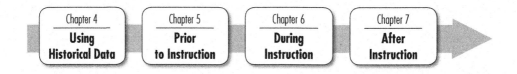

Section 3: Considerations Beyond the Tier 1 Classroom

The last section of the book examines decisions that exist beyond the Tier 1 classroom. The chapters in this section acknowledge and address the mutually dependent relationship between individual teachers and district-wide and school-wide considerations.

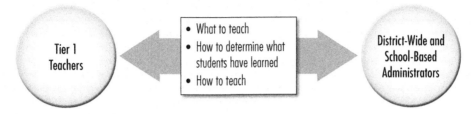

At the end of this process lies the potential of a multi-tiered system of supports that maximizes every student's chances of achieving academic proficiency.

Section 1
Foundations of Tier 1—Standards, Effective Practices, and Data

An effective Tier 1 curriculum and assessment system requires attention to several critical instructional variables—what to teach, how to teach, and how to determine what students have learned. Chapters 1 through 3 examine several of these sometimes-neglected variables that can impact success for the full range of students in the Tier 1 classroom.

Standards—whether state or national—provide the framework for what students should know and be able to do at each grade level. Chapter 1 sets the instructional stage by examining the role of standards. With standards defining the content of curriculum, the next critical variable is to plan lessons that are based on effective instructional practices. Effective practices speak to how content and skills are conveyed to students. Chapter 2 takes a look at these practices against the backdrop of teacher knowledge of content and skills. Cognitive preparation, the intentional use of this knowledge by teachers, emerges as the essential link for the appropriate selection and use of effective instructional techniques. Within the context of what to teach and how to teach it, data collection provides the evidence of success for both the teacher and students. Chapter 3 focuses on a survey of the data options—what to use, when to use it, and how data inform the instructional decision-making processes on behalf of all students.

Together these three chapters are designed to provide the necessary background for the creation of an effective Tier 1 program.

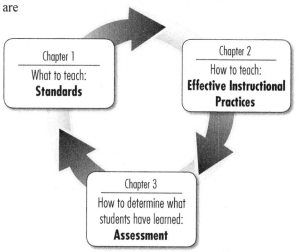

Chapter 1
What to teach:
Standards

Chapter 2
How to teach:
Effective Instructional Practices

Chapter 3
How to determine what students have learned:
Assessment

CHAPTER ONE

Standards—The Foundation of a Successful Tier 1 Program

The Case for Standards-Based Instruction

In a strong Tier 1 context, high value standards drive the creation of a logical scope and sequence of instructional objectives, which in turn drive the development of day-to-day lessons and tasks designed to build concepts and skills. When there is a tight link between standards and classroom content, students engage in tasks that prepare them for success on standards-based assessments. The following graphic (Figure 1.1) shows the relationship among standards, instructional objectives, lessons, and the assessment feedback.

FIGURE 1.1

```
                              Standard
                                │
        ┌──────────────────────┼──────────────────────┐
        ▼                      ▼                      ▼
┌──────────────────┐  ┌──────────────────┐  ┌──────────────────┐
│ Instructional    │  │ Instructional    │  │ Instructional    │
│ Objective        │  │ Objective        │  │ Objective        │
└──────────────────┘  └──────────────────┘  └──────────────────┘
        │                      │                      │
        ▼                      ▼                      ▼
┌──────────────────┐  ┌──────────────────┐  ┌──────────────────┐
│    Lessons       │  │    Lessons       │  │    Lessons       │
└──────────────────┘  └──────────────────┘  └──────────────────┘
        │                      │                      │
        ▼                      ▼                      ▼
              Ongoing Assessment
```

Let's take a look at an example (Figure 1.2) of this relationship among a Grade 5 Common Core State English/Language Arts standard, possible instructional objectives, and lessons to develop the content and skills.

FIGURE 1.2

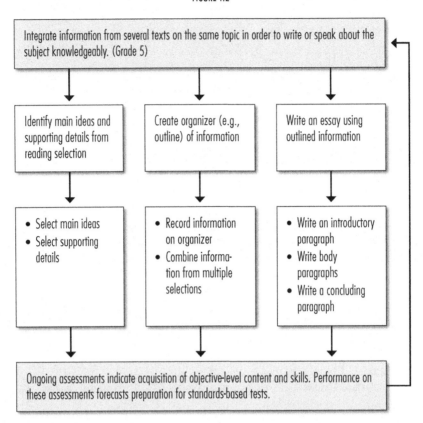

Performance on formative assessments forecasts successful performance on standards-based state assessments. In other words, as Elmore suggests (2010), the tasks anticipate the expectations of the accountability measure, increasing the likelihood that the results on these measures will be positive. In this example, the lessons should develop students' ability to integrate information from several sources to write knowledgeably about the subject.

Determining High Value Standards

When designing an effective Tier 1 program, then, we start with standards. As of this writing, more than forty states have adopted the federally developed Common Core State Standards. This appears to indicate that the move toward national standards is here to stay. However, even if this were not the case, teachers have been expected for some years to teach academic standards set forth by individual states. Standards for English language arts and mathematics—whether state or national—designate what students should know and be able to do at specific grade levels. A vital step in designing strong Tier 1 instruction is knowing what standards to teach, when to teach them, and when to assess them. These standards provide the framework for an articulated scope and sequence of instructional objectives across classrooms and grades, as well as the basis for designing or selecting a curriculum. In this way, the standards form the foundation from which Tier 1 teachers plan their daily instruction.

As logical as this process sounds, it is not an easy task. The development of standards is as much a political as an educational enterprise. Committees comprised of educators as well as representatives of special interest groups commonly develop standards. In an effort to take everyone's "must haves" into account, standards development committees often come up with a dizzying number of standards in a particular subject area. As Marzano (2003) notes, trying to focus on all the standards would require students to go through the "22nd grade."

What are educators to do when attempting to manage an overwhelming number of standards? Fortunately, there is an answer to that question. Not all standards are created equal. Within the universe of standards, school districts must identify "high value" standards to determine what to emphasize in the classroom. While there is a legitimate place for a certain percentage of standards that educators consider important but are not amenable to state testing, instructional content must include these high value standards. Since state tests signal important learning outcomes, state test samples, maps, and blueprints provide insight about essential, or "high value," standards. Therefore, examining test questions is one way to identify areas of emphasis in terms of both content and the way in which students will be expected to demonstrate that knowledge. Whatever approach is used to review and rank the importance of standards, teachers and administrators must work together to establish a collection of high value standards that guide the development of a scope and sequence of content/skills.

The Blueprint: A Logically Designed Scope and Sequence

The presence of high value standards is one hallmark of appropriate content for the Tier 1 classroom. Another is a scope and sequence of content and skills that form a blueprint for instructional objectives and lesson activities designed to help students succeed with standards-based assessments.

Why is a well-developed scope and sequence important? Attention to the dependent relationship of skills—both within and across grades—is vital to cumulative and successful student achievement. Poorly sequenced content and skills run the risk of students developing a knowledge base that has holes in it like "Swiss cheese." Unfortunately these holes can have a cumulative and compounding negative impact on student learning across the years.

Just as important as a well-developed scope and sequence is a commitment to following it. If teachers deliver idiosyncratic content based on personal preferences rather than on the logic of cumulative content and skill development, students and teachers face challenging situations at successive grade levels. Consider the following illustration (Figure 1.3). The top row of circles represents three first grade classes with students represented by letters. When teachers stick to the scope and sequence in first grade (row one)—that is, they teach the instructional objectives for the grade level—there will be consistency in what students will know as they advance to the next grade level (row two). If first grade teachers fail to teach concepts/skills assigned to that grade level, second grade teachers will have to deal with learning gaps as the students are regrouped into second grade classes. Rather than moving forward with the second grade curriculum, they will have to spend time filling in the holes created by instructional variance in first grade or forge ahead and ignore skill gaps. As troubling as this phenomenon is in the primary grades, these holes compound as students move through subsequent grades 3–12. Ultimately, failure to pay attention to logical scope and sequence of instructional objectives contributes to curriculum casualties (Greene, 1998; Gickling, 1985), that is, students who have content and skill "holes" resulting from teachers' varying practices.

FIGURE 1.3

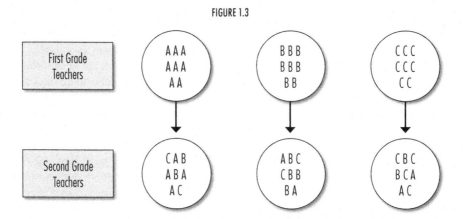

The first steps, then, in creating a strong Tier 1 classroom are identifying high value standards and establishing a logical scope and sequence derived from high value standards. These steps establish <u>what</u> teachers should teach and the order in which to teach it.

The Case for a Curriculum

While an analysis of standards and the related scope and sequence form the basis of what to teach, it is a curriculum based on that foundation that enables teachers to carry standards into the classroom. Whether purchased from an outside source or developed locally, such a curriculum ensures that several things can happen. First, this curriculum frees teachers to focus on teaching rather than on the search for or development of materials. While it is *possible* for teachers to develop instruction in alignment with the standards, it isn't *practical* on a day-to-day basis. Stanley Pogrow (1998) likened the expectation that teachers develop curriculum on the fly to "asking an actor to perform Shakespeare—but to write the play first." Second, a well-designed curriculum fosters continuity of instructional focus within and across grades and schools. Third, a thoughtfully developed curriculum emphasizes deeper knowledge of content, which is an essential ingredient of effective teaching. As we will explore in the next chapter, an in depth knowledge of content and skills allows for more creative and strategic delivery of instruction based on students needs. Such a curriculum is the vehicle that translates standards and scope and sequence into classroom instruction.

Teaching the Standards to Meet the Needs of All Students

While a common curriculum provides an essential starting point, teachers must still plan *how* daily instruction can meet the needs of all students. This is the reality of teaching *the students in front of us* rather than delivering instruction as though all students have the same needs. When we analyze the standards in light of the mandate to reach all students through Tier 1 instruction—whether students are advanced, proficient, or require additional intervention—it becomes imperative to consider the range of acquisition, that is the extent to which students can or will be able to acquire the content, concepts, or skills encompassed within a standard. Not every student will acquire the same breadth and depth of knowledge with all of the standards. Therefore, instruction can be thought of in terms of the extent to which students, grouped according to proficiency level, will acquire designated standards. Each standard can be taught and learned to different degrees of acquisition, as illustrated below.

FIGURE 1.4

Degree of Standards Acquisition

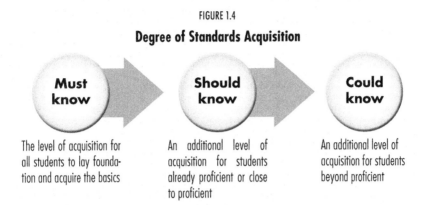

The level of acquisition for all students to lay foundation and acquire the basics

An additional level of acquisition for students already proficient or close to proficient

An additional level of acquisition for students beyond proficient

The level of acquisition of standards forms the basis for differentiating instruction. In this model, instructional planning combines the level of standards-based knowledge with student need.

The "*must know*" level pictured in Figure 1.4 provides essential understanding of standards for all students. When planning for instruction, the teacher must ask how she can teach the basic concept to everyone in her class. For some students, she will design tasks that promote basic conceptual understanding that leads to more complex grade level work. For others, the Tier 1 teacher's challenge is to help them build concept knowledge while prerequisite skills are being taught in Tiers 2 or 3. In *must know* instruction, it is not the Tier 1 teacher's job to remediate skills that are already targeted in Tier 2 or Tier 3. Instead, her instruction takes into account that such students will be able to apply that knowledge at grade level once their basic skill level increases. For example, a student may be able to grasp the concept of long division with supplementary materials but will only be able to perform long division once the prerequisite skill of borrowing is learned in Tier 2 or 3. Or a student can learn the concept of point of view using supplementary materials and then be able to apply that knowledge at grade level once their reading skill has increased as a result of Tier 2 or Tier 3 intervention. This is the promise of RtI. As we teach standards-based concepts, the students that receive additional assistance in the form of targeted interventions beyond Tier 1 will eventually be able to apply that knowledge with grade level material.

"*Should know*" is standards-based instruction applied at grade level and includes a more in depth acquisition of a particular standard. The planning for the teacher includes the question—"What should the student know and be able to do in order to remain or become proficient?" This is a critical step in the process if we recognize that a strong Tier 1 is the cornerstone of an effective RtI system. We do not want to lose our proficient and advanced students because we are only focusing on those who struggle. The *should know* category is also the basis for Tier 1 interventions applied at grade level so that students who seem to have the prerequisite skills to perform proficiently but are not grasping either a new concept or skill are provided with short term Tier 1 intervention within the core class.

The "*could know*" category of instruction provides enrichment and extension beyond the grade level standards for students who have demonstrated proficient and advanced knowledge of grade level work. This group includes but is not limited to our gifted students, who are often left out when districts implement RtI. When planning, the teacher includes the question: What could the students know if I let them go? At this level we design more independent, focused work that provides students with the opportunity to develop deeper and more sophisticated understanding of all the standards and allows them to move beyond grade level with supplementary materials, research, and projects.

The levels of Marzano's new taxonomy (Marzano and Kendall, 2008) provide teachers with a guideline to design tasks with different cognitive requirements (Table 1.1).

TABLE 1.1

Levels of the New Taxonomy

Level 1
Retrieval: recognizing and recalling

Level 2
Comprehension: integrating

Level 3
Analysis: matching

Level 4
Knowledge Utilization: investigating

Level 5
Metacognition: Monitoring clarity

Level 6
Self System: Examining motivation

Proficient and advanced students require tasks that allow them to develop deeper knowledge of the standards beyond the grade level requirement. A caution—the goal for "*could know*" is greater depth, not just more work. Elmore (2010) illustrates this point in the following example: *Students are studying the periodic table of elements. Advanced students are required to memorize the table.* The latter task does not demand that advanced students acquire a deeper knowledge of the periodic table of elements; it merely keeps students at the lowest level of taxonomy—recognizing and recalling information. In contrast, if students were required to investigate some aspect of the organization of the periodic table, they would be developing a deeper knowledge.

The following table (Table 1.2) illustrates the distinction between "*must know*," "*should know*," and "*could know*" for an English Language Arts standard, as well as the progression of the standard across the elementary, middle, and high school levels.

TABLE 1.2

Sample English/Language Arts Standard

	Elementary	Middle School	High School
Level of Acquisition	Describe characters in a story (e.g., their traits, motivations, or feelings) and explain how their actions contribute to the sequence of events (G3)[1]	Describe how a particular story's or drama's plot unfolds in a series of episodes as well as how the characters respond or change as the plot moves toward a resolution (G6)	Analyze how complex characters (e.g., those with multiple or conflicting motivations) develop over the course of a text, interact with other characters, and advance the plot or develop the theme. (G9–10)
Must know how to	Describe traits, motivations, or feelings and what actions show. (Use simpler text or pictures if necessary to establish concepts)	Describe the series of episodes of a story that lead to a resolution of the plot. (Use simpler text if necessary to establish concepts)	Describe the multiple or conflicting motivations of a main character in a story or drama and how they relate to the plot or theme development. (Use simpler text if necessary to establish concepts)
Should know how to	Describe all three criteria and be able to specifically cite examples of actions that contribute from the story at grade level.	Describe how characters respond or change through a series of episodes as the plot moves toward a resolution.	Describe how the multiple or conflicting motivations of a complex character interact with other characters to develop the plot.
Could know how to	Describe more subtle indicators of the criteria from inference and analysis; identify the same elements in more difficult text.	Analyze the factors that cause changes in the characters through the evolution of the plot.	Analyze the relationship between the multiple or conflicting motivations of a complex character and those of other characters to develop the plot or theme.

[1]From the Common Core State Standards for English Language Arts, 2010

This view of standards provides a basis for differentiating instruction in both whole and small groups. Differentiation is not arbitrary; it is developed relative to what we know about our students, as well as to the complexity of the standard. To teach standards to all students, the goal is the same: help all students learn the "high value" standards to the "*must*," "*should*," or "*could*" levels, depending on their current and potential skill levels. Differentiation can adjust the process and the product but not the destination: mastery of the essential standards at the *must know* level and the opportunity to extend learning to *should know* and *could know* levels.

Practical Application: Reflecting on the Standards

You will need English/Language Arts standards and the curriculum scope and sequence used by your school district.

Activity

- Identify high value standards for your grade level.

- Examine the existing curriculum scope and sequence. Determine if it is a standards-based scope and sequence.

- Discuss next steps to ensure alignment between the scope and sequence and the high value standards.

- Determine the "must know, should know, and could know" level of standard acquisition for the high value standards.

CHAPTER TWO

The Case for Cognitive Preparation for Instruction

The first step in creating an effective Tier 1 program is arranging high-value standards into a logically designed sequence of skills and concepts. With the curriculum in place, the next step is to plan lessons that incorporate effective instructional practices. This is the *how* of teaching, and the *how* goes a long way toward determining whether students acquire the content and skills outlined in the curriculum. No matter which of the myriad delivery models and research-based strategies and materials we select and use in the Tier 1 classroom, teachers' knowledge about content and skills provides the essential foundation to teach, assess, and adjust instruction. Cognitive preparation, the intentional act of utilizing this knowledge, emerges as a common denominator of effective instructional practices to reach the needs of all students.

Instructional Anticipation: The Starting Point

Cognitive preparation for teaching is what Lemov (2010) in *Teach Like a Champion* calls "no-short cuts preparation." When teachers devote time to thoughtful preparation, they not only anticipate what might be challenging in the lesson, but also identify how to tailor instruction to the diverse needs of their students. Whether teachers are developing their own lessons or following a published teacher edition, examining and understanding the knowledge base of the lessons are essential to promote student learning. Elmore et al (2010) contend that "increases in student learning occur only as a consequence of improvements in the level of content, teachers' knowledge, and skill (p. 23)." This type of cognitive preparation for instruction is essential for teachers to be able to "pivot" when student response varies from the expected, a strategy that we will look at more closely in Chapter 6.

Prerequisite knowledge targeted for specific populations, such as English Learners, is referred to as front-loading the language of the lesson (Dutro & Moran, 2002). In a Mastery Learning model, we refer to this instructional step as pre-teaching. Anticipation of prerequisites, no matter what we call it, is an area of instruction that has helped educators move beyond a silo approach (i.e., instruction limited to specific programs or populations) to differentiate support. A focus on prerequisite knowledge contributes to meeting particular student needs regardless of program designations, such as ELL, SPED, or gifted. For example, English Learners can benefit from strategic attention to vocabulary by linking new words to cognates from their first language. On the other hand, instructional anticipation that focuses on what the lesson is trying to accomplish makes it possible to ask probing questions of students with advanced skills to activate the discovery of new concepts. At the heart of this process is careful previewing of the content load for a lesson—the skills, vocabulary, and concepts—in order to identify the possible instructional hooks. These hooks are important because we learn by linking something new to what we already know. New knowledge, that is something "unknown," builds upon the known.

The following table (Table 2.1) illustrates the use of pictures, graphic organizers, and content links to bridge known to unknown learning.

TABLE 2.1

When the lesson will require students to ...	Frontloading can ...	Example
Learn new vocabulary	Develop prior knowledge of vocabulary terms to make acquisition of new knowledge easier. Use of pictures or realia can facilitate the process	If students are learning the literary term **mood**, frontloading could focus on a series of face illustrations conveying moods (e.g., a smiling face, a sulking face, a sad face). If students are learning the math term **variable**, pre-teaching could focus on the multiple meanings of the word that are familiar to students prior to explaining the math-specific meaning (i.e., a letter representation of a number in an equation).
Learn a new process	Review strategic key prerequisite skills and discuss where that might lead	If students are learning the Final "**e**" spelling rule, review the v<u>ce</u> pattern for base words. (e.g., **bake/baking**; **hope/hopeful**)
Learn the structure of a paragraph	Use a graphic organizer to visually represent how the organization of sentences can turn into a paragraph.	If students are learning the components that make up the structure of a paragraph, use a graphic organizer to visually illustrate each component — topic sentence, body sentences, and concluding sentence.
Expand content knowledge	Ask questions to tap what students already know	If students are learning to read a map, ask students to name landforms and link how the key on a map represents the landforms
Identify innuendo and inference	Prior to progressing to inference and innuendo	Review a series of cartoons from a daily newspaper to identify inference and innuendo conveyed through the cartoon content. Move to instruction in political cartoons.

Repeated instructional backtracking to fill in information or to review skills serves as a red flag that the teacher must attend more thoughtfully to prerequisite content or skills. The more side trips we make during instruction to clarify or review, the less efficient our instruction will be. As we will discuss in Chapter 5, when pre-assessment data is available, it can confirm the need for pre-teaching. Considering the skill and knowledge base of students facilitates both instruction and learning. This process also defines the limits of the Tier 1 teacher's responsibilities for teaching all prerequisite skills versus those that are taught through Tier 2 or 3 interventions.

The Task-to-Results Match

A task-to-results match is another way in which we can facilitate success for students. This pre-planning approach looks at tasks, namely instructional activities, in terms of their contribution to outcome measures, that is results. Elmore (2010) puts it this way, "If the tasks do not reflect the expectations of the external accountability system, or our best ideas about what students should know and be able to do, then we should not expect to see the results reflected in external measures of performance." To examine this match should not be confused with teaching to specific test items. On the contrary, teachers' examination of test items provides them with an awareness of test makers' expectations and helps them prepare students for those expectations.

As teachers work to develop content knowledge, it is important that they provide students with practice demonstrating their knowledge and skills in ways that match test makers' expectations. Students often make progress in their day-to-day assignments and study, but the way in which questions are asked on tests throws them a curveball. As educators, we can mitigate this problem by helping students learn to answer questions similar to those they will encounter on tests. By designing some of our day-to-day questions using the type of academic vocabulary and syntax found on tests, students are better equipped to negotiate questions on tests. Consider the difference in the wording of these questions using classroom talk and academic vocabulary and syntax:

TABLE 2.2

Classroom Talk	Academic Vocabulary and Syntax[1]
Where do aardvarks live? A. Egypt B. Libya C. Gabon D. Kenya	In which of the following countries would an aardvark most likely make its home?[2] A. Egypt B. Libya C. Gabon D. Kenya
What did Tim Connor think about failure? A. There is no excuse for failure. B. Some risks are not worth taking. C. Instead of avoiding failure, people should learn from it D. For every story of failure, there is a story of great success.	Which statement best expresses Tim Connor's attitude toward failure?[3] A. There is no excuse for failure. B. Some risks are not worth taking. C. Instead of avoiding failure, people should learn from it. D. For every story of failure, there is a story of great success.
How is Document A organized? A. Identification of a problem followed by a solution B. Presentation of a main idea followed by supporting details. C. Criticism of opponent's position point by point. D. Description of causes and effects of a certain issue.	What is the main pattern of organization used in Document A?[3] A. Identification of a problem followed by a solution B. Presentation of a main idea followed by supporting details. C. Criticism of opponent's position point by point. D. Description of causes and effects of a certain issue.

[1] Actual examples from state assessments released items
[2] www.ade.az.gov
[3] www.cde.ca.gov

While these pairs of questions are asking for the same information, the vocabulary choice and syntactic complexity of the examples in the right hand column make the readability level higher and more difficult. Students often have learned the content and skills but fail to fully demonstrate their knowledge when tested, not because they lack knowledge, but because they are confused by the way in which questions are asked.

It is equally important to align the content emphasis of our instruction with high value standards. For example, if students spend a lot of the year engaged in literary analysis but the majority of the questions on standards-based assessments focus on comprehending and interpreting informational text, our instruction has not paid attention to the task-to-results match. Consequently, we have failed to prepare students for success.

Gradual Release of Responsibility—The Teacher to Student Transfer

The gradual release of responsibility is a research-based instructional model in which the responsibility for task completion shifts from the teacher to the students. Researchers have documented this model as an effective approach for improving writing achievement (Fisher & Frey, 2003), reading comprehension (Lloyd, 2004), and literacy outcomes for English learners (Kong & Pearson, 2003). Teachers gradually reduce support as students demonstrate success. Conversely, teachers might increase support and differentiate instruction when students struggle. The following graphic (Figure 2.1) shows the level of scaffolding as responsibility is released.

FIGURE 2.1

Proportion of Responsibility for Task Completion

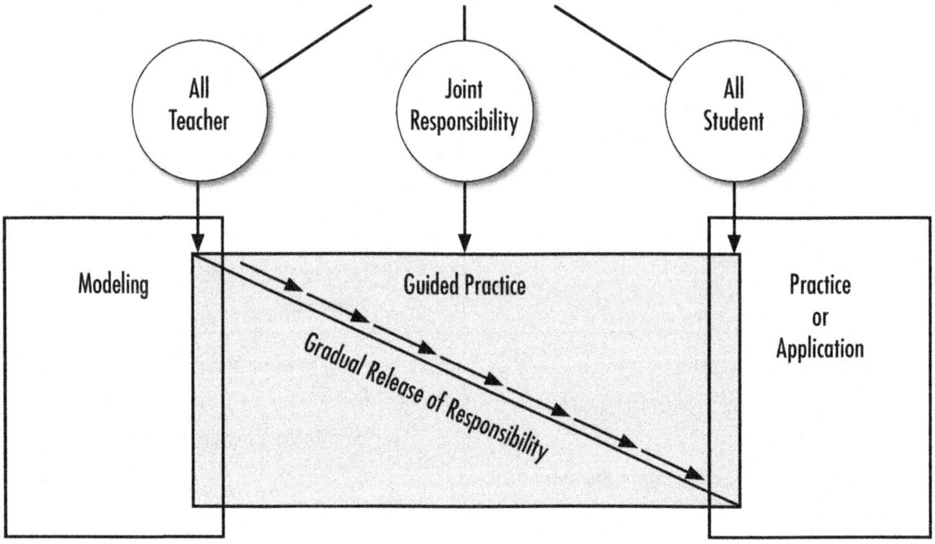

Used with permission
Pearson and Gallagher, 1983

The purpose of this approach is to teach in what Vygotsky (1962) calls the zone of proximal development. This zone assures the proper ratio of known to unknown content and skills—roughly 80%—for students to benefit from instruction. But how do we determine whether or not students are performing in this zone? Data—observational data, error analysis, and performance on formative assessments—indicate whether students are performing in the targeted range.

The emphasis in the gradual release model is on the amount and duration of explicit instruction and scaffolding. Performance information prior to, during, and after instruction, tells us how much modeling or practice students need before releasing them to more independent practice and application. For example, if students make many errors, the teacher should continue modeling and offer more guided practice. If students make few errors and raise few clarifying questions, the teacher can release them to a less-scaffolded level of support.

Grouping

The mention of grouping often strikes fear in teachers' hearts. Unfortunately, grouping conjures up concerns ranging from management issues to implications of tracking. To accomplish the goals of differentiated instruction, however, it is critical to group students according to their needs and the purpose of the small group activity. Effective grouping must be data based, flexible, and adjusted frequently.

The amount of grouping necessary depends on the composition of the class. The more homogeneous the class, the less grouping is required. Conversely, the more heterogeneous, the more grouping is needed. As discussed by Vygotsky, the point of grouping is to have students working in their "zone" as much as possible. This maximizes instructional time for teachers and learning time for students.

Grouping can fit into the instructional process at any point, such as front loading, discussion, and re-teaching strategic skills. The purpose of grouping is to match the size and composition of the group with the purpose of the instruction. The following table (Table 2.3) provides examples of this match.

TABLE 2.3

	Front loading	Discussion	Re-teaching
Purpose	Increase student access to content instruction for English learners by anticipating and pre-teaching language demands	Enhance student engagement by increasing participation and interaction among students	Provide strategic skill instruction to address a pattern identified through error analysis
Target composition of the group	Students with varying degrees of prior knowledge	All students in the class grouped in dyads or triads	Students whose work showed an error pattern

Engaging Students in Instruction

The goal of all instruction is to engage students actively in their own learning (Guthrie & Wigfield, 2000). Without students' participation and on-task behavior, learning does not happen. Teachers promote student engagement with appropriate selection of instructional techniques and materials, as well as efforts to make the content lively and relevant. When we talk about the zone of proximal development, this applies not only to the difficulty level of the material, but also to the extent to which students see the purpose in what they are studying and learning. Elmore (2010) makes an important distinction between student compliance and interest. The former suggests on task behavior; the latter suggests cognitive engagement. As discussed in Chapter 1, attention to levels of learning—"must, should, and could" know—is a critical variable in meeting students at their level of interest and in their "zone."

Gickling and Armstrong (1978) in their seminal research studied the relationship between on-task behavior and instructional match. They found that off-task behavior occurred as frequently when students were bored as when frustrated. Christenson and Ysseldyke (1989) identified both the rate of academic responding along with an appropriate instructional match as important instructional variables with strong links to achievement. According to their research, students gained the most from their learning time when materials were at an appropriately matched difficulty level, that is their instructional zone, so that they had a high rate of successful responses indicating understanding of the content (Gettinger & Seibert, 2002).

Keeping these points in mind, we can use a range of strategies to increase student engagement (Table 2.4). The first list Participation and Practice, provides examples of strategies that elicit surface levels of participation by ensuring that all students are actively participating. The second list, Interest and Involvement, focuses on strategies that encourage a deeper level of participation by attending to students' interests and instructional range (Vygotsky (1962); Gickling, (1978). Both are important in order to fully engage students.

TABLE 2.4

Participation and Practice	Interest and Involvement
Choral read with students	Relate instruction to students' lives
Provide the opportunity for choral repetition and response with purpose	Activate student interest
Randomly select students to answer questions	Assign tasks within the students' zone of proximal development (instructional match)
Provide additional examples and modeling before independent work	Assign tasks that span the range of "must know," "should know," and "could know"
Create opportunities for partner work	Partner and group projects and investigation.
Focus on ratio of known to unknown to maximize learning	

Providing Feedback

A teacher's content and skill knowledge is critical to the process of providing effective feedback. Such knowledge makes it possible to maximize the teachable moment when student errors occur during instruction or to identify patterns of errors in student work; at the same time, it makes feedback both timely and appropriate. The more the teacher knows, the greater the insight that emerges from students' errors. Feedback exists along a continuum from error analysis of discrete skills to observations of patterns of understanding (or misunderstanding) while students work. Frequently asked student questions during a lesson may indicate the need to cycle back in a lesson to re-teach or re-explain content or skills.

The goal when providing feedback is to advance students' knowledge and skills, not just to provide the right answer. To guide students to a correct answer or understanding requires that teachers can draw upon the necessary content to help them arrive at the right answer. The following example by Lemov (2010) illustrates this correction process.

> "If a student can't read **might**, the best way to correct such a decoding error may be to improve her knowledge of the rules. After all, she's likely to struggle with **sight** and **tight** as well. Rather than saying, "That word is **might**," the teacher might say, "**i–g–h–t** says 'ite.' Now try that word again." This has two benefits: it requires the student to incorporate the new information and then decode the original word successfully, and it reinforces a rule she can use on other high-frequency words. The next time the teacher corrects, he or she might say, "**i–g–h–t** says …?" and ask the student to recall and then apply the rule. In most cases, asking students to self-correct by applying a rule or new information—"that vowel is a long **a**. Now try that word again," is another typical example—is powerful because it addresses the cause, not just the symptom, and thus contributes to a long-term solution." (Lemov, 2010)

While this example may seem simple, it is designed to show the difference between supplying an answer and guiding students to understand the answer for future application. Other examples occur in Chapter 6, During Instruction. This process is as important with broad concept development as for discrete skills. At the heart of corrective feedback is the teacher's knowledge of the content in order both to identify the nature of the problem and to provide links to guide the student to the correct response. Central to a teacher's ability to provide effective feedback is careful monitoring through frequent checks for understanding. The importance of careful monitoring cannot be overstated. Schmoker (2010) reminds us that, "The consistent delivery of lessons that include multiple checks for understanding may be the most powerful, cost-effective action we can take to ensure learning."

Threshold of Tier 1

Teachers who use the instructional practices presented in this chapter will maximize student learning within the Tier 1 curriculum. If students struggle to achieve mastery-level performance with these practices in place, it may be a sign that students have hit their threshold in Tier 1. Often the culprit is students' weaknesses in basic skills; their skills simply aren't strong enough to give them access to core content without accommodations. Such students, regardless of age, require skills-based instruction, usually in English/ Language Arts. Skills-based instruction is the purpose of Tiers 2 and 3 interventions.

Practical Application: Inventory Your Strategies

- Think about your classroom instruction and the effective teaching practices presented in this chapter. Use the chart to organize what you currently do.

	Task-to-results match	Engage students	Provide feedback
What do you do now?			
How is it working?			

- Identify areas of instructional practice that you would like to improve. Focus on these as you continue with this book.

CHAPTER THREE

What's Data Got to Do With It?

A coherent curriculum, based on high-value standards and knowledge of the tools to differentiate that curriculum for all learners, provides the bedrock for a successful multi-tiered system of supports. Within that system, data collection is the engine that drives teachers' decision-making processes about students. Data help educators determine instructional need, adjust the pacing of content, and measure growth. The universe of data is large; the teacher's task is to select the appropriate data for specific purposes. The purpose of this chapter is to survey the types of data teachers need to make instructional decisions. The application of that data is the focus of subsequent chapters.

Types of data
★ make instructional decisions

Using Data: From Global to Specific

Data include a wide array of information about learning and range from global tests of achievement to discrete measures of skill or content acquisition. Global measures include the types of instruments used for state tests. They provide broad-based information about student and program performance best suited to school or district accountability needs. In contrast, skill inventories, fluency probes, and error analysis supply the specific information required in the classroom to inform day-to-day instructional decisions.

The assessment process is effective and efficient when it helps us look at student performance from a global to an increasingly more specific level of information within and across tiers. It is helpful to think of the global to specific use of assessment as a funneling process. Let's consider this "funneling" analogy applied to the screening process, which in the RtI model is intended to identify students at risk for academic failure (Figure 3.1). At the most global level, annual state assessments identify students requiring a closer look. Suppose that this data, often based on predetermined performance ranges, suggest that a student falls into an "at risk" category. Additional assessments are then needed to verify this determination. For example, a comprehension test is used to confirm that understanding reading material is a problem. Skill specific assessments, such as vocabulary, fluency, or decoding, zero in further on the type and intensity of instructional support the student needs. The most specific information, such as that gathered from skill specific assessments, pinpoints the instructional needs of individual students.

FIGURE 3.1

Reading Comprehension Test

Screening

Skill Specific Assessment

INSTRUCTIONAL PLACEMENT

The Terminology Conundrum

Despite the frequent reference to data use in the instructional process, it is easy to become confused by the tangle of terminology. For example, while working with a large urban district, we witnessed a lengthy discussion about the district's assessment needs, only to realize that different constituencies had different understandings about the meaning of screening, benchmarks, and other terms that had been bandied about. To avoid confusion and provide clarity, we are providing a brief description of some assessment types frequently cited for use in RtI (Table 3.1)

TABLE 3.1

Assessment type	Description
State tests	Determines learning of state standards
Standards-based benchmarks	Provides interim performance data towards meeting criteria on state tests
Screeners	Identifies students at risk for academic failure
Diagnostic assessments	Provides specific information about the cause of learning problems
Inventories	Examines student's knowledge of content and skills in specific subject areas; often used before instruction begins
Curriculum-based measures	Provides information to monitor students' growth in basic academic skills usually in the form of short, repeated fluency measures
Curriculum-based assessment	Provides information from observations and samples of performance tied to the taught curriculum
Chapter tests	Provides information about what students learn at chapter-length increments of the curriculum specific to text
Error analysis	Uses detailed analysis of student work to identify patterns of content or skill misunderstanding

Assessment tools are generally classified into two main groups: criterion-referenced or norm-referenced. Criterion-referenced assessments measure knowledge and understanding in relation to what is to be learned, namely specific standards of performance. These assessments measure what students are learning in relation to the standards. On the other hand, norm-referenced tests compare a student's performance to that of an appropriate peer group (i.e., a norm group). Both types of measures provide information about an individual student. Criterion-referenced measures allow comparison to a standard (i.e., a specified level of performance). Norm-referenced measures allow comparison to other students of similar age or grade. For example, identifying if students can read a paragraph at a rate of 120 CWPM is criterion referenced. In contrast, how students read a paragraph compared to other 5th graders requires a norm-referenced perspective. Both types of assessment tools can be standardized, meaning that the tools are administered in the same way each time the tool is used. The same, or standardized administration, ensures that the results of the assessments are obtained from comparable administration conditions. The assessments we focus on in this book fall into two main categories as illustrated in the following diagram (Figure 3.2).

FIGURE 3.2

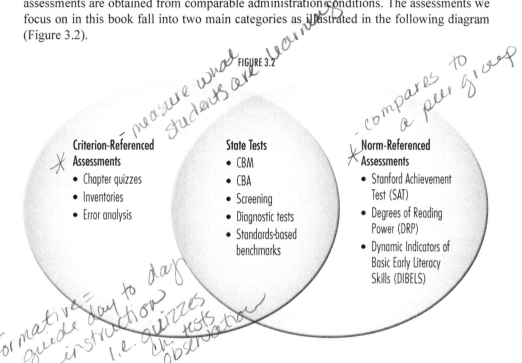

(handwritten annotations:) - measure what students are learning · compares to a peer group · Formative = day to day guide day to day instruction i.e. quizzes ch tests observation

Criterion-Referenced Assessments
- Chapter quizzes
- Inventories
- Error analysis

State Tests
- CBM
- CBA
- Screening
- Diagnostic tests
- Standards-based benchmarks

Norm-Referenced Assessments
- Stanford Achievement Test (SAT)
- Degrees of Reading Power (DRP)
- Dynamic Indicators of Basic Early Literacy Skills (DIBELS)

We can also classify assessments according to their role in instruction. Formative assessments drive the teacher's day-to-day decision-making process. These data sources, such as observations, quizzes, tests, and error analysis of class work, provide information to adjust teaching and learning during the instructional process. In contrast, summative assessments are administered periodically to gauge student learning in relation to content standards or units of curriculum content. As such, summative assessment is foundational for both accountability and program evaluation. This level of data drives curricular and program decisions.

(handwritten annotations:) Summative = gauge learning of standards or curriculum

Focus on Purpose

Although assessments are typically designed with a particular use in mind, the reality is that the same assessment tool can be used for different purposes. Rather than focusing on the search for the perfect instrument, the question to ask is, "What do I need to do with the data?" Table 3.2 illustrates this point and labels the Tiers (1, 2, 3) for which the instrument is appropriate.

TABLE 3.2

What Type of Assessment Tools Can Serve This Purpose?

(Note: Numbers in columns refer to Tiers 1, 2, or 3)

Purpose	State tests	Standards-based benchmarks	Screeners	Diagnostic assessment	Skill Inventories	Curriculum-based measures	Curriculum-based assessment	Chapter quizzes	Error analysis	How used
Screen: Identify potential candidates for intervention (i.e., predict an outcome months or years in advance (National Center on Learning Disabilities (NCLD) website)	1		1							• Establish cut points using proficiency categories • Establish performance guidelines based on local data patterns
Diagnose: Determine why individual students fail to respond to intervention				3						• Target specific areas of weakness to probe unresponsiveness to instruction
Inform instruction and intervention: Identify patterns of strengths and weaknesses		1		1 2		1	1		1 2	• Plan instruction, intervention, and grouping based on patterns of performance
Inform instruction: Determine learning rate						1 2 3				• Adjust pacing; consider referral to RtI team if the rate is persistently slow.
Inform instruction: Match materials to students' performance level							1 2 3			• Ensure that materials are available at a range of readability levels; use instructional match to keep students "in the zone"
Inform instruction: Identify skills for re-teaching or enrichment						1 2 3	1 2 3	1 2 3		• Establish performance criteria (e.g., 80%) • Display student data graphically to monitor performance • Identify skill progress against desired progress • Identify the pattern of performance from student work
Monitor progress: Answer accountability questions	1 2 3		1 2 3							• Measure change in learning over time

In an era of budgetary constraints juxtaposed against escalating requirements for accountability, resourcefulness is not only desirable it is necessary. Focused selection and use of assessment tools supports the adage that more is not necessarily better in terms of making data based instructional decisions. For this reason, selecting assessment tools according to needs is important to avoid unnecessary duplication of data or gaps in necessary data.

Tier-Specific Purposes for Data

Data function to inform instruction in all tiers. However, each tier has data requirements unique to that tier, largely because teachers at each level must make different kinds of decisions. The following graphic (Figure 3.3) illustrates how the purpose of data differs according to tier.

FIGURE 3.3

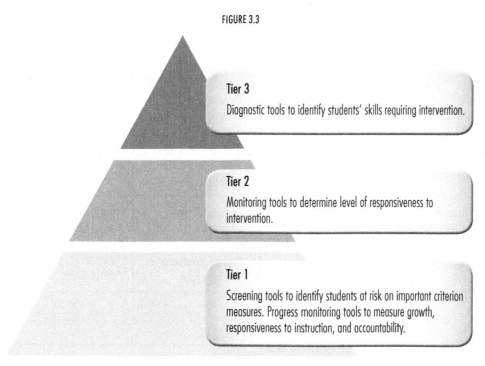

Tier 3

Diagnostic tools to identify students' skills requiring intervention.

Tier 2

Monitoring tools to determine level of responsiveness to intervention.

Tier 1

Screening tools to identify students at risk on important criterion measures. Progress monitoring tools to measure growth, responsiveness to instruction, and accountability.

As the need for more instructional intensity becomes evident, the assessment instruments become more fine-tuned to pinpoint weaknesses in basic skills.

Different Decisions, Different Data

Multiple sources of data provide distinct levels of information about what, when, and how to teach. That said, not everyone within the district or school community uses the wide range of assessment tools in the same way. Instructional decision-making plays out differently depending on roles. The following table (Table 3.3) illustrates this variation.

TABLE 3.3

Who Uses What?

	District leadership	School leadership	Classroom teacher
State tests	• Accountability purposes • Program design consider-ations	• Accountability purposes • Establish/tailor school-based priorities	• Tie instruction to broad performance goals
Standards-based benchmarks	• Directs emphasis in cur-riculum decisions • Identifies focus of profes-sional development	• Directs emphasis in cur-riculum decisions • Identifies focus for profes-sional development	• Determine how performance relates to instructional planning
On-going assess-ments	• Supports selection of instructional materials with valid assessment components	• Understand to support selection of instructional materials • Understand to include in teacher observation protocol • Use to determine areas requiring professional development resources	• Use for instructional plan-ning pertaining to pacing, grouping, differentiation
Error analysis; observational information	• Awareness level	• Support professional development • Include in teacher observa-tions and identification of coaching support	• Use for daily instructional planning and corrective feedback as part of the instructional process and differentiation

Predictable Patterns of Assessment

For a Tier 1 teacher, a global assessment is initially helpful for identifying students who are in the "at risk" range for academic failure. As the year progresses, however, the teacher must turn to a regular pattern of assessments to determine if "at risk" students are on a trajectory for successful performance on state tests. The results of a predictable cycle of assessments inform the intensity and focus of instruction (Figure 3.4).

FIGURE 3.4

	September	October	November
Assessment Process	Screening	Ongoing	Ongoing
How does this inform instruction?	Identifies students at risk for academic failure who need further diagnostic investigation	Informs how well students are getting the content and skills being taught	Informs how well students are getting the content and skills being taught

	December	January	February
	Screen (Benchmark)	Ongoing	Ongoing
	Checks if students are on trajectory for State test. Identifies students moving into an at risk range.	Informs how well students are getting the content and skills being taught	Informs how well students are getting the content and skills being taught

	March	April	May	June
	Screen (Benchmark)	Ongoing	Ongoing	End of Year Summative
	Checks if students are on trajectory for State test. Identifies students moving into an at risk range.	Informs how well students are getting the content and skills being taught	Informs how well students are getting the content and skills being taught	Informs how students' learning is progressing in relation to content standards or course goals

Managing the Data You Have

Selecting the appropriate assessment instrument for a specific purpose is an important piece of data-driven instruction. Yet data are not useful without the means to organize and manage the information the data yield. Tracking student progress is a vital part of instruction. Documentation is crucial to determining need and eligibility for service in a multi-tiered system. Previous data provide the baseline for student performance for the upcoming year. Current data, collected, reported and analyzed in an efficient manner, measure student progress from that baseline.

Data must be in an accessible, teacher-friendly format if teachers are to analyze the information efficiently. District-generated or integrated online systems can serve this purpose. Let's look at a couple of examples. In Figure 3.5, educators in the district identified the essential information required to place students in appropriate instructional programs. The sample articulation card illustrates a district-generated approach to data management. Adapted with permission from Hawthorne School District in California, the sample articulation card (Figure 3.5) illustrates a streamlined and highly focused data management approach. Initially the district used 3 x 5 cards to capture the information. Eventually they converted the format into an electronic data system that has worked efficiently to address their data management needs. A sample data set based on their format is displayed in Figure 3.5. All of the data in this example comes from the previous school year: state outcome assessments (A), comprehension screen (B), English Language proficiency designation (C), and Special Education status (D). Student performance on standards-based benchmarks (E) provides a more detailed layer of information to guide planning.

FIGURE 3.5

Standards Based Benchmark Assessments

			Benchmark 1	Benchmark 2	Benchmark 3
(A) State test band Level 4: Proficient	Strand				
	Vocabulary		2	4	3
(B) Comprehension Screen Lexile: 630	Comprehension		2	1	2
	Grammar		4	3	5
(C) Eng. Prof. EL 4	Writing		5	3	4
(D) SPED: no	Standard based concepts		3	3	3
Tier 2: no Tier 3: no			**(E)**		

Documentation

In addition to the value of data management for the purpose of analysis and interpretation, a systematic approach to managing student-specific information is essential to the RtI process. If, in fact, a decision is made to refer a student to the RtI team, the teacher must justify that decision and provide documentation of the student's lack of progress based on Tier 1 instruction even though the student has been provided with differentiated instruction to address this lack of progress. This documentation should include but is not limited to:

- Curriculum based assessment results illustrating lack of progress over four consecutive data points.
- Articulation of the types and duration of differentiation implemented to improve student performance.
- Identification of the student's strengths and weaknesses to date.
- Samples of student work.

With the information in hand, the step of documenting student performance and progress is more manageable and more easily transferred to any required referral form when a student's profile suggests a more in depth look by the RtI team. Based on the information provided on the form, the RtI problem solving team decides whether the evidence is enough to warrant further assessment and the need for Tier 2 or Tier 3 services.

Cut Points, Trend Lines, and Other Decision-Making Guidelines

No matter the source of data, ultimately teacher and leadership teams must agree upon how to interpret the data. Cut points, trend line rules, and other decision-making guidelines help data users determine what the data mean and how it will be used.

In the context of the RtI model, data interpretation is inextricably linked to the determination of need for more instructional time and greater instructional intensity. The more discrepant student performance is from expectations for mastery of the core curriculum, the greater the need. Figure 3.6 depicts this relationship of time, instructional intensity, and distance from the core.

FIGURE 3.6

Tiers As a Function of Instructional Time and Instructional Intensity

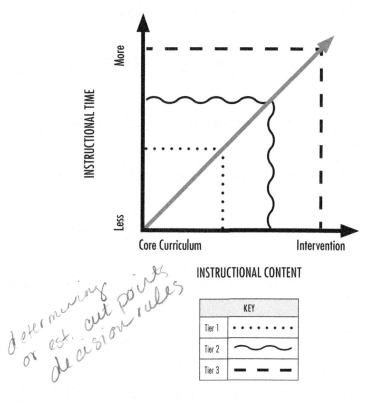

Cut points define the performance levels to be used for various classification purposes. For example, educators frequently use cut points to define the performance criteria from screening data for each tier in a multi-tiered system. The following table (Table 3.4) provides an example of how the cut points for tier designation differ for grade ranges from kindergarten through grade 12.

TABLE 3.4

Cut Points by Grade Range for Tier Designations

	K – 2	3 – 5	6 – 8	9 – 12
Tier 1	• At or above grade level • > 50%ile on normative measures		• At or above grade level • > or = 50%ile on normative measures	
Tier 2	• Within 1.5 – 2.0 years of grade level • 30 – 50%ile on normative measures		• Between 4th grade and current chronological grade level • 30 – 50%ile on normative measures	
Tier 3	• More than 2 years below grade level • < or = 30%ile on normative measures		• < or = to 4th grade level • < or = 30%ile on normative measures	

local needs v[?]
& national
scores

The use of normative measures is important to ensure that critical decisions are based on an external criterion that is not referenced only to the class in which the student is enrolled. Determination of need for more intensive intervention should be related to national norms rather than to the group of peers students happen to be with. It is important to keep in mind that determining cut points requires that a district interpret the national norms and decide how best to apply them to local conditions.

Cut points in the form of performance bands can also be used to distinguish between a class-wide versus student-specific performance issue. Such distinctions can play an important role in the allocation of resources and the focus of instruction. For example, the performance of class members in Figure 3.7, suggests a class-wide problem with digit recognition on a math CBM with a large number of students falling at the low end or below the target range. This pattern suggests the need for more practice or re-teaching for the whole class. In contrast, Figure 3.8 shows only a couple of students falling below the targeted range, suggesting student-specific intervention. The first situation requires an instructional solution; the second more likely necessitates additional teacher resources.

FIGURE 3.7

Math CBM—Mr Jones' 7th and 8th Grade Class

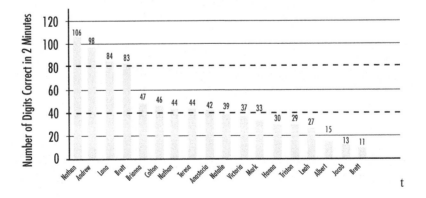

t

FIGURE 3.8

Math CBM—Mr Jones' 7th and 8th Grade Class

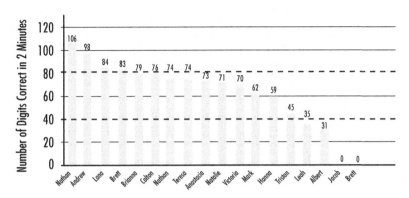

Another way to characterize performance discrepancy is to use Chall's (1983) stages of reading development. Table 3.5 shows the relationship between the stages of reading development, the corresponding grade level for those stages, and performance on a comprehension measure, Degrees of Reading Power (DRP). Ideally the relationship between the grade level corresponding to the stages and performance on the assessment measure are in alignment as illustrated on the top chart. When, however, the stage of reading development for a student does not correspond with his/her grade level (Table 3.6), the difference is the discrepancy that must be addressed instructionally.

TABLE 3.5

Chall's Stages of Reading Development	Grades Associated With Stage	DRP Scores Associated With Grade
Stage 5: Reading to Construct New Knowledge	Post-High School	
Stage 4: Read for Multiple Viewpoints	High School Grades 9–12	> 67
Stage 3: Reading to Learn	Grades 4–8	43–66
Stage 2: Confirmation and Fluency	Grades 2–3	21–42
Stage 1: Alphabetic Decoding	Late Kindergarten— Early Grade 2	< 20
Stage 0: Pre-Reading and Emergent Literacy	Kindergarten	

TABLE 3.6

Chall's Stages of Reading Development	Grades Associated With Stage	DRP Scores Associated With Grade
Stage 5: Reading to Construct New Knowledge	Post-High School	
Stage 4: Read for Multiple Viewpoints	High School Grades 9–12	> 67
Stage 3: Reading to Learn	Grades 4–8	43–66
Stage 2: Confirmation and Fluency	Grades 2–3	21–42
Stage 1: Alphabetic Decoding	Late Kindergarten– Early Grade 2	< 20
Stage 0: Pre-Reading and Emergent Literacy	Kindergarten	

Trend line rules are effective for interpreting ongoing data, particularly for data gathered in Tiers 2 and 3 where intervention is provided. For this approach to data interpretation, the teacher collects at least eight data points over four weeks to determine a trend, or slope, line. In this approach, a trend line of current performance is compared to a goal line. If the trend of performance is steeper than the goal line, the decision-making response is to raise the goal. If the trend of performance is less steep than the goal line, the teacher needs to make an instructional change.

Another approach to data interpretation is the "four point rule," which lends itself to the type of student performance information gathered in Tier 1 (Lembke, 2010). Similar to trend lines, the "four point rule" indexes performance against a goal line. With this approach, the educator examines the most recent four data points across a period of multiple weeks. For example, if an 8th grade science teacher targets fluent recognition of vocabulary in her class and sets 80 CWPM (correct words per minute) as the goal, student performance can indicate the need for adjustment in instruction. If all four data points are below the goal line (Figure 3.9), the teacher knows she needs to change instruction, or she may use this snapshot of data as a red flag that a student's needs should be reviewed by an RtI team. If all four points are above the goal line (Figure 3.10), the teacher should think about changing the goal. If data points are both above and below the goal line (Figure 3.11), the instructor should continue with the current instructional plan.

FIGURE 3.9

Science Vocabulary Words CWPM

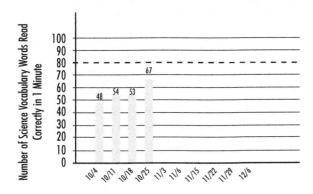

The **goal line** represents a desired (targeted) rate of improvement. The goal line provides a level of performance useful for individual student planning and with aggregated student data for accountability purposes.

FIGURE 3.10

Science Vocabulary Words CWPM

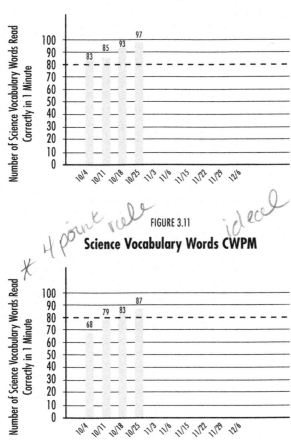

FIGURE 3.11

Science Vocabulary Words CWPM

✱ 4 point rule   ideal

In determining response to instruction or intervention, trend lines and the four-point rule provide critical information about discrepancy—and discrepancy is at the heart of the decision-making process. Determining the level of difference and rate of learning difference signals the need for more intensive support and potential referral for special education (Batsche, et al., 2006). In addition to the use of online systems, it is possible to calculate a discrepancy ratio quantifying the difference between desired and actual levels of performance (Rosenfield, 1987).

Some performance areas do not lend themselves to discrete data points. Rubrics work well for these areas. They allow teachers to describe the traits of performance along a continuum of pre-determined criteria for performance. While less quantifiable, a rubric is well suited for more complex tasks, such as writing essays, required of older students to meet state standards.

Now What?

Inventorying and selecting assessment tools to provide data for instructional decision-making should be based on the information a particular tool provides, the level of detail needed, and on a cycle of use. Teachers need to keep the following "Do's" and "Don'ts" in mind as they make decisions and use data.

Do	Don't
Use data from multiple sources to document performance and make decisions	Make decisions based on a single point of information. No tool is that perfect. The implications are too important to relegate a decision to such a limited data set.
Focus on function. Figure out what you need to know and do and determine if you have the tools needed to address that need.	Focus on finding the perfect test.
Consider efficiency when selecting tests. When possible, chose group tests.	Use individually administered tests when a group test can yield the same information.
Come to agreement and use the same terminology in your school or district. Be sure to define your terms.	Assume that everyone has the same understanding of the terminology surrounding assessment.
Manage streams of data to make analysis efficient.	Become buried in data without a system of management.
Establish a schedule for using data. Make it an integral part of the day-to-day operation of instructional planning and decision-making.	Put data away. Out of sight data is data that doesn't get used.

Practical Application: Inventory Your Assessment Tools

Activity

Inventory your assessment tools and procedures by purpose. Use the table below. What do you use? What do you need? Use the tables on pages 30–32 as you do this activity.

Purpose	Kinds of assessment tools and procedures
Identify potential candidates for intervention	
Identify patterns of strengths and weaknesses for a whole class	
Determine learning rate	
Match materials to students' performance level	
Inform instruction = identify skills for re-teaching or enrichment	
Answer accountability questions	

Section 2

Practical Application—From What to How

Section 1 provided information and direction about developing an effective Tier 1 curriculum and assessment system. Now we take the next step—practical application. While it is critical to know what to do to improve Tier 1 instruction, it is equally important to know how and when to do it. It has been our experience that most teachers have access to data but often do not know how, or do not have time, to use it in a way that helps them determine student need, respond to that need, and identify the threshold of Tier 1. Section 2 (Chapters 4-7) takes teachers through the assessment and instruction process. Each section begins with the type of data that are useful at specific times before, during, and after instruction. The graphic below shows the linear progression of instruction and the points in time when data can be used to guide instruction. Each chapter will focus on a specific time in the instructional process.

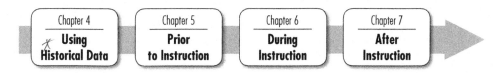

In each chapter, we have provided examples of data use before giving readers an opportunity to work through the cycle of instruction and assessment using their own data. In order to facilitate application and practice, chapters 4-7 follow the sequence shown (below).

It is our hope that the information, examples, classroom scenarios, and practice opportunities assist teachers in developing data-based Tier 1 instructional practice that meets the needs of all students.

CHAPTER FOUR

Using Historical Data to Plan Initial Instruction

We know that high value standards, instructional objectives derived from those standards, and careful attention to a coherent scope and sequence and curriculum form the foundation of an effective Tier 1 program. To make that program work, however, requires the implementation of a cycle of instruction and assessment that makes use of data from multiple sources. If using data is a prerequisite for instructional planning, what can we do to prepare for the students in front of us before they walk in the classroom door? This is the time we know least about them. In fact, we haven't met them yet. The answer is that data from previous years provide insights into what our students know and are able to do. In other words, students in grades three through twelve come to us with academic histories that allow us to make instruction more effective for students and more efficient for teachers from day one. An examination of this historical data sets the stage for a repeating cycle of instruction and assessment in Tier 1.

Data Source: Historical Student Data

Four historical data sources, displayed below, are particularly useful before the year begins. Each provides insight into past student performance and sheds light on future instructional need. Not all of the sources and results listed below may be accessible to all teachers, but using whatever historical data do exist makes Tier 1 instructional planning easier right from the beginning.

example MAP?

FIGURE 4.1

State or National Assessment	Standard Based Benchmark Assessments	Screening Assessments	Demographics
Standards based assessment administered once per year at various grade levels	Standards based assessments given periodically through the year	Normed referenced reading assessments	Information collected about the characteristics of students
Results are usually available before the beginning of the school year	Assess a predetermined number of standards in the scope and sequence	Assess student reading or math level, given to some or all students three or more times per year	Information is self-reported or the result of assessments
Student performance relative to the previous year's standards	Student acquisition of standards over a period of time	Student growth in reading or math over the previous year	Accommodations, EL strategies and language level, intervention, culturally relevant instruction

Some of the data report general levels of achievement but may also include detailed information including performance on specific information broken down by literacy strand, skill, or question type. Specific demographic information reports the makeup of the incoming class so that we can teach *all* the students in front of us.

How Does the Data Inform Instruction?

Data from the previous year provides insight about students that will be in our class. Although there are multiple ways to use any data set, we have matched each data source to one or more specific teacher responses in order to provide a concrete connection between data analysis and instructional planning. The following chart connects each data source to the various actions teachers can take in light of that data.

FIGURE 4.2

State/National Standards Based Assessments	• Develop a RtI class triangle • Identify students who may need further assessment by the RtI team
Historical Standards Based Benchmark Assessments	• Document student patterns of strength and weakness from the previous year
Historical Screening Assessments	• Inform choice of appropriate supplemental materials • Inform initial group formation for differentiated instruction
Demographics	• Identify considerations for specific populations • Choose culturally relevant materials

National and State Test Data

Tier 1 instruction is based on grade level standards. It stands to reason, then, that the Tier 1 teacher benefits from knowing to what extent students have learned standards-based skills and concepts from the previous grade. Indeed, Batsche, et al (2006) cite "progress toward standards" as one of the important components of an RtI assessment system. State/national assessment data reveal the performance range of students in a teacher's class and become part of cognitive preparation for future instruction. Additionally, it helps to identify students who may need further investigation by the RtI team providing that they are not already receiving intervention. We want to make sure that we identify students in need of intervention as early as possible in a school year so that intervention services are provided in a timely manner.

Classroom RtI Triangle

One way to concretely look at a class from a standards perspective is to create an individual class RtI triangle based on student performance on the state/national assessment from the prior year. State boards of education identify broad performance bands and cut points for those bands. Students' scores place them in bands that identify how close or how far they are from proficiency. The following examples depict state performance bands from two states and describe the process of turning those bands into an RtI triangle for a teacher's incoming class.

Example 1: California—California defines its standards-based bands as Advanced, Proficient, Basic, Below Basic and Far Below Basic. These band designations provide a starting point to help develop a Tier 1 classroom RtI triangle.

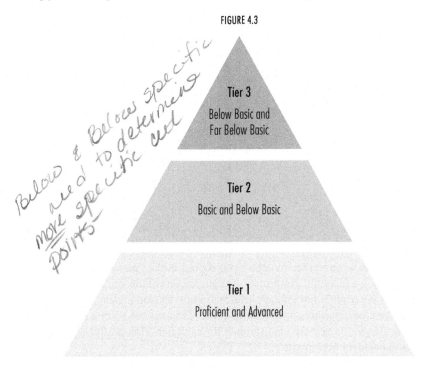

FIGURE 4.3

Tier 3
Below Basic and
Far Below Basic

Tier 2
Basic and Below Basic

Tier 1
Proficient and Advanced

Below & Below specific need to determine more specific cut points

Figure 4.3 illustrates an RtI triangle based solely on the state of California assigned proficiency bands. Notice, however, that band designations are not clear enough to determine exact student performance. We have five bands and three tiers. In order to fit the five bands into the three tiers of the RtI triangle, decisions are made to align the band performance with the tiers in the RtI triangle. This may be a district, school, or grade level team determination. Proficient and advanced performance obviously indicate that Tier 1 instruction is sufficient. Far Below Basic performance identifies students who are performing significantly below grade level. However, Basic and Below Basic performance are a bit ambiguous. In this instance, the school needs to review the Basic and Below Basic categories and develop more specific cut points which would then result in a clearer triangle depiction of student performance.

Example 2: Texas—Texas performance bands, on the other hand, identify students whose performance on TAKS (Texas Assessment of Knowledge and Skills) is characterized as "did not pass," "passed" and "commended." Based on this information, a Texas Tier 1 classroom RtI triangle would look like the figure below.

FIGURE 4.4

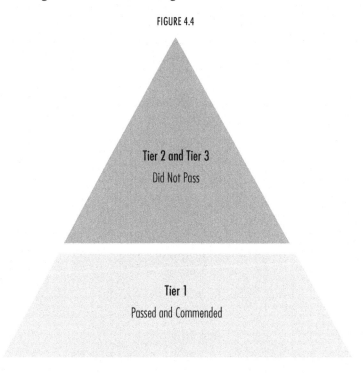

Tier 2 and Tier 3
Did Not Pass

Tier 1
Passed and Commended

Although we can assume that students who scored in the "passed" or "commended" range are proficient, we have little information about the rest of the students other than they did not pass. This is certainly not enough information to develop a clear picture of student performance. Therefore, teachers and administrators examine the score range of students that did not pass TAKS to determine cut points for each tier. This creates a more realistic picture of current student performance.

Use the Triangle for Instructional Planning

Developing class triangles without purpose is a rather useless exercise. However, taking that information and using it to set goals, guide instruction, and identify student needs turns this activity into a useful tool in the process of cognitive preparation for instruction. The following example—Ms. Young's class—demonstrates how to use the RtI triangle for instructional planning.

The RtI triangle for Ms. Young's class (Figure 4.4) tells her that she needs to prepare for a range of learners. Not only will she have to address the needs of students who have previously performed below standard, she will also have to account for students who are coming into class at proficient and advanced levels of performance and design instruction to keep them proficient and advanced. Constructing a triangle allows Ms. Young to immediately identify individuals who may require differentiated instruction. She will likely need challenging tasks for those students working at the *should know* and *could know* levels in order to keep them engaged and interested. On the other hand, some of the struggling students, ones who are receiving Tier 2 or Tier 3 services, may need additional help to reach the *must know* and *should know* levels of standard acquisition.

In addition to informing her teaching preparation, the RtI triangle alerts Ms. Young that two students, Mary and Joshua, may require Tier 3 services. Their test data indicate subpar performance, and they are not receiving additional intervention. In light of this, she considers reporting their names to the RtI team so that it can further investigate Mary's and Joshua's needs.

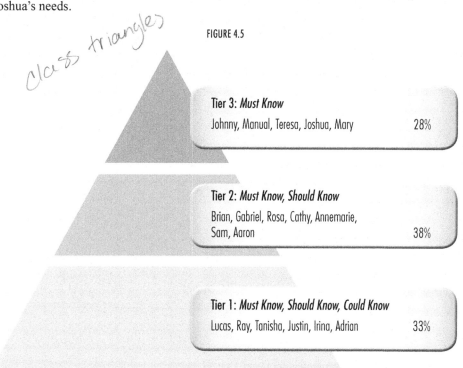

class triangles

FIGURE 4.5

Tier 3: *Must Know*
Johnny, Manual, Teresa, Joshua, Mary   28%

Tier 2: *Must Know, Should Know*
Brian, Gabriel, Rosa, Cathy, Annemarie,
Sam, Aaron   38%

Tier 1: *Must Know, Should Know, Could Know*
Lucas, Ray, Tanisha, Justin, Irina, Adrian   33%

Ms. Young realizes that her triangle does not match the optimum triangle (80-15-5) discussed in the introduction. In addition to identifying student need, it assists her in developing instructional goals that will move her class closer to the ideal proportions.

① student need
② set instructional goals

Practical Application: Create Your Own Baseline Triangle

You will need recent state test results or standards-based benchmark assessments for your class.

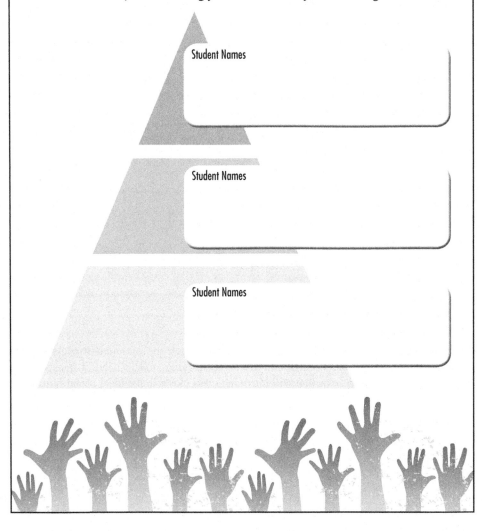

Activity

Using your recent test data, construct a beginning-of-the-year class triangle for your Tier 1 class. In constructing a baseline triangle:

- Place students within the tiers of services according to your cut points.
- Think about the type of preparation and resources that you will need to serve your students.
- Identify students who may need further investigation by the RtI team.
- Set goals for your first assessment cycle (benchmark, periodic assessment) that will bring you closer to the optimum configuration.

Student Names

Student Names

Student Names

Standards-Based Benchmarks — *add'l benchmark layer 1 point of info* [handwritten]

In addition to state assessment results, the previous year's standards-based benchmark assessments provide an additional layer of information useful for planning instruction for the upcoming year. The benchmarks represent a student's performance at specific points during the school year while the state assessment represents performance on a single day. It is worthwhile to compare the results of both to develop a more complete portrait of an individual student's achievement. Reviewing students' previous benchmark assessments helps the teacher identify patterns of strength and weakness for individual students and across a class. Consider the following examples:

Example 1: The articulation card below represents a middle school student's benchmark performance over the previous year. Each benchmark assesses a different set of standards from the district's scope and sequence. The scores are reported by standard strand. A score of 4 or higher denotes proficient performance. Analysis of the scores shows that this student, while at or close to grade level in some strands, has significant weakness in comprehension as evidenced by consistently low scores in comprehension.

TABLE 4.1

Previous Year's Standards Based Benchmarks

Strand	Benchmark 1	Benchmark 2	Benchmark 3
Vocabulary	2	4	4
Comprehension	2	1	2
Grammar	4	3	5
Writing	5	3	4
Standard based concepts	3	3	3

If the pattern of weakness depicted above is unique to this one student, the teacher will differentiate comprehension instruction so that the student can reach the "should know" level of standards acquisition. However, if the same pattern occurs across a group or class, the teacher will have to restructure her Tier 1 instruction to include a heavy emphasis on explicit comprehension strategies.

look for patterns of weakness [handwritten]

Example 2: This fourth grade student's articulation card illustrates his previous year's benchmark performance. In this particular school, five benchmark assessments are tied to instructional units and reported by strand. When reviewing the student's scores, it becomes clear that this student performed at advanced levels by the end of last year. Through analysis of this data, the teacher realizes that she will have to develop tasks for this student that provide additional depth within and beyond the grade level standard. In other words, the teacher must push the student toward the *could know* level of standards acquisition.

TABLE 4.2

Standards-Based Benchmark Assessments

Strand	Unit 1	Unit 2	Unit 3	Unit 4	Unit 5
Vocabulary	4	5	4	4	5
Comprehension	4	4	5	4	5
Grammar	4	3	5	5	5
Spelling	5	5	5	5	5
Writing	4	5	5	5	5
Fluency	4	5	4	5	5

Using historical Tier 1 data provides important and useful insight. Teaching is not a generic one-size-fits all endeavor. Each year our students come to us with different needs, and each year we must design instruction that meets those diverse needs.

The following activity will help teachers identify individual student and class needs.

Practical Application: Determining Patterns of Strengths and Weaknesses

You will need the previous year's standards-based benchmark assessment data.

- Review standards-based benchmark assessments for four of your students.
- Write the names of students and list any strengths and weaknesses for each.
- Identify the instructional planning response for each student.
- Identify patterns of performance and discuss possible instructional approaches to meet the needs of your class.
- Create a larger chart to include your entire class.

Class Profile

Student Name	Student Strength	Student Weakness	Instructional Response

Screening Results

Screening results are helpful in choosing supplemental materials as well as in designing group configurations for differentiated instruction. Part of a teacher's preparation for an incoming class includes the selection of supplemental materials to facilitate student learning. Although Tier 1 curricular materials are written at grade level, the use and choice of supplementary materials offers opportunities to teach standards-based concepts and skills to our very highest and very lowest performing students. For our high performing students, such materials provide the opportunity to apply and extend their knowledge with reading material targeted to their level. Additionally, the use of supplementary materials targeted to the grade level of struggling students allows them to learn important concepts while their literacy skills are being addressed in Tier 2 or Tier 3.

FIGURE 4.6

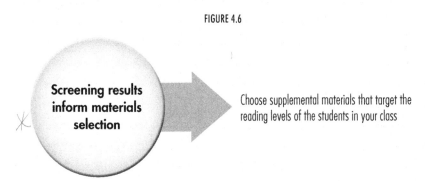

Screening results inform materials selection

Choose supplemental materials that target the reading levels of the students in your class

Another benefit of reviewing student screening data is that it assists in determining initial group configurations. Tier 1 teachers use flexible small group instruction for numerous reasons ranging from concept discussion to Tier 1 intervention. The teacher assigns students to small groups based on the task to be accomplished. Access to content is one function of small group instruction. Knowing students' reading comprehension levels allows the teacher to create small group instruction for re-teaching, reinforcement, and enrichment for *must know*, *should know*, and *could know* levels of standards acquisition. Students do not remain in static small groups throughout the year—hence the word flexible. However, when students require material to provide access to or beyond the core, grouping by comprehension level leads to differentiated instruction that serves students in a manner that meets their needs. The critical point is that small group configurations are based on relevant data, not guesswork.

FIGURE 4.7

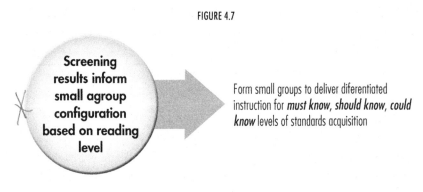

Screening results inform small agroup configuration based on reading level

Form small groups to deliver diferentiated instruction for *must know, should know, could know* levels of standards acquisition

The choice of supplementary materials and group configuration at the beginning of the year is part of the cognitive preparation for teaching. Using previous screening data ensures that teachers make choices based on realistic information about students. Whether forming heterogeneous groups for discussion or homogeneous groups for differentiation, data is the basis for successful grouping and supplemental materials choice.

Practical Application: Determining Grouping Configurations and Related Needs for Supplementary Materials

You will need screening results from the previous year.

Activity

- Determine criteria/range for differentiated instruction in small groups.
- Using historical screening results, construct groups according to those reading levels.
- Identify supplementary materials that can be used with each group.
- Use this chart as a sample. Create a larger chart to include your whole class.

Student Name	Comprehension Level	Supplementary Materials

Demographics

Assessment data is only part of a student's story. Teachers teach the whole child and that means digging deeper than recent test scores. Demographic data informs instructional planning based on student characteristics. Such information is usually available through the school or district office and can help to round out our picture of the students we teach.

Understanding the characteristics of the students in an incoming class helps teachers plan instruction that respects the individual needs of students relative to their talents, backgrounds, and challenges. It allows us to personalize instruction beyond test scores and can result in student engagement and success. How to address all the characteristics of individual students in a Tier 1 class is certainly challenging but a little investigation can result in more thoughtful instructional planning. The table below identifies on site help that teachers can use to become more informed about the students in class.

TABLE 4.3

Characteristic	What does it mean for instruction?	Who can help?
Special Education Students Including Gifted	• Provide accommodations according to the student's IEP.	• Special Education Teacher • School Psychologist
Gifted Students	• Provide work that challenges the gifted student.	• Teacher of Gifted Students • School Psychologist
English Learner	• Provide specifically designed instruction according to the student's language acquisition level.	• English Language Development Teacher
Students receiving Tier 2 or Tier 3 intervention	• Differentiate by process and product for **must know** and **should know** concepts in Tier 1 instruction. • Identify skills being addressed in intervention groups.	• Intervention Teachers • Gifted Teachers
Culture	• Design culturally responsive instruction and be able to relate instruction to students' lives and background experiences.	• The student, other teachers, parents, researchers.

Practical Application: Considering the Diverse Populations in Your Class

You will need demographic data for students in your incoming class. Use the following table to chart that data.

Activity

- Make a list of the demographic characteristics of the students who will be in your upcoming class.
- Identify what information you will need to plan and who has that information.
- Based on your class demographics, identify three ways that your future instruction will need adjustment.
- Create a larger table to chart the results for your entire class.

Student Name	Culture	EL Status	IEP Services	Intervention Services	Who Should I Talk To?

Multiple Layers of Data

This chapter identified four kinds of data and how to use that data in planning instruction for a class at the beginning of the year. However, determining the type of services a student may need is not as simple as looking at one assessment and then making a decision. As discussed in Chapter 3, data can be used in multiple ways to refine and confirm decisions made about student progress and need. Let's use the development of a class RtI triangle as an example of how those sources can be combined to help Ms. Young make a more informed decision about Joshua.

Joshua: A Case Study—Based on the results of the state assessment, Ms. Young determines that Joshua, a 6th grade student, should be referred to the RtI team for further investigation. However, before making that referral, Ms. Young reviews all of Joshua's data from the previous year. The data provided on the articulation card below includes the following information.

- State test results by band.
- Strand specific results from last year's benchmark assessments (score range of "1 to 5" with "5" being highest).
- Comprehension screen given to all students at the end of the previous year.
- Special considerations: (EL, SPED, Intervention, Culture).

TABLE 4.4

Joshua: 6th Grade, California Standards Based Benchmark Assessments

State test band	Strand	Benchmark 1	Benchmark 2	Benchmark 3
Level 1: Far Below Basic:	Vocabulary	2	4	5
Comprehension Screen Grade Level: 5.5	Comprehension	2	1	2
	Grammar	4	4	5
	Writing	5	4	4
Eng. Prof. EL 4 Culture: Hispanic SPED: no Tier 2: no Tier 3: no	Standard based concepts	3	3	4

Notice that Joshua's overall performance data does not match the results of the state assessment. Joshua's screening assessment shows that his comprehension level is within half a year of grade level. His benchmark assessments show overall proficiency, but we notice that there is a marked difficulty in comprehension as evidenced by scores of 1 and 2 across the year. We also see that Joshua is a level 4 English Learner. The question is, then, should Ms. Young change her decision to refer Joshua to the RtI team.

TABLE 4.5

Joshua: 6th grade

Assessment Results	Implications	Referral to RtI Team
State Test: Far Below Basic	Student is performing significantly below grade level on State Test	Yes
Screen: 5.5 grade level	Student is slightly below grade level but classroom differentiation may be sufficient.	No
Benchmarks: Overall good performance with marked difficulty in comprehension	Differentiation for this student should focus on comprehension strategies.	No
English Learner: Level 4	Student will receive ELD services this year. Focus should be comprehension.	No Communicate this information to the ELD teacher.

Ms. Young knows that one data source is never enough to refer a student to intervention. Based on her analysis, Ms. Young's changes her decision to refer Joshua to the RtI team. The state test results in combination with additional data show that Joshua should be in range of proficient performance in Tier 1 with focused comprehension instruction, continued ELD services, and close monitoring. Ms. Young's thorough data analysis ensures that she is now better prepared to meet Joshua's needs in Tier 1. *need for small group*

A review of pertinent data is always critical when constructing instructional plans but *re* it becomes even more crucial when we are determining if a student is in need of more or less intervention. Recognizing that data provides layers of insight helps us to refine both *comp.* our instructional and intervention practices in a multi-tiered system. Use the following articulation card to determine if the student should be referred to the RtI team for further investigation.

Practical Application: What Does the Data Tell You?

Review the following articulation card: Based on the data available, make the following decisions.

1. Should this student be referred to the RtI team for further investigation? Ask yourself:

    a. Do the data fall into your school or district's cut points for intervention? If so, which Tier?

    b. Is the instruction and differentiation strong enough in Tier 1 to bring this student to grade level without additional intervention?

    c. Does the student already receive additional time with a Special Educator?

2. What are the instructional implications for this student in the Tier 1 class?

Gabriela: 9th Grade Texas
Standards-Based Benchmark Assessments

State test band	Strand	Benchmark 1	Benchmark 2	Benchmark 3
Level 1: Passed	Vocabulary	2	1	3
Comprehension Screen Grade Level: 7. 0	Comprehension	3	2	2
	Grammar	3	2	2
	Writing	3	2	2
Eng. Prof. English Only Culture: White SPED: yes Tier 2: no Tier 3: no	Standard based concepts	3	2	2

Every piece of information that we can learn about our upcoming Tier 1 class contributes to effective teaching and learning. While some teachers prefer to "get to know" students on their own, thinking of students as blank slates puts both the students and the teacher at a disadvantage. Learning as much as possible about students helps teachers design successful instruction before the first day of school.

CHAPTER FIVE

Before Instruction

Let the Teaching Begin

Reviewing student data before the year begins provides a global picture of student performance with which to plan initial lessons. That picture gets refined as we move through the actual process of instruction, assessment, and adjustment in the presence of students. If we launch directly into instruction, we often discover that some of the students already know the content or know less than we thought. We have all heard the response to a new concept: "We already did this!" However, just because I've heard of a persuasive essay and may even be able to define it, doesn't mean I can write one. Once the school year is underway, determining student knowledge (pre-assessment) before new instruction is more efficient than trial and error.

Data Source: Pre-Assessments *- Brief informal*

Pre-assessment, especially in grades 3–12, can be complicated due to increasingly complex concepts and skills required in the higher grade levels. To deliver effective Tier 1 instruction, teachers need insight into the breadth and depth of what students already know and are able to do. Bear in mind that we don't expect students to know everything about what we are going to teach. If that were the case, we could just move to the next unit. However, we have to know if our lesson plans, as written, are going to leave students frustrated, confused, or bored. It is easier to adjust lesson plans at the beginning than to backtrack later. It is important to note that pre-assessment in Tier 1 is not designed to identify the kinds of skill discrepancies addressed in Tier 2 or Tier 3 interventions.

Pre-assessment tools in Tier 1 are usually brief, informal ways to find out what students know and don't know (Gusky, 2010). Clearly, it is better for students to know more rather than less when they encounter new concepts. The ability to connect new content with prior knowledge is invaluable during instruction. While many pre-assessment methods and instructional responses are available in education, we will focus on a few in order to illustrate the use of pre-assessment in the instructional cycle. The following graphic describes the information provided by each type of measure and identifies whether the information provides quantifiable or anecdotal results.

FIGURE 5.1

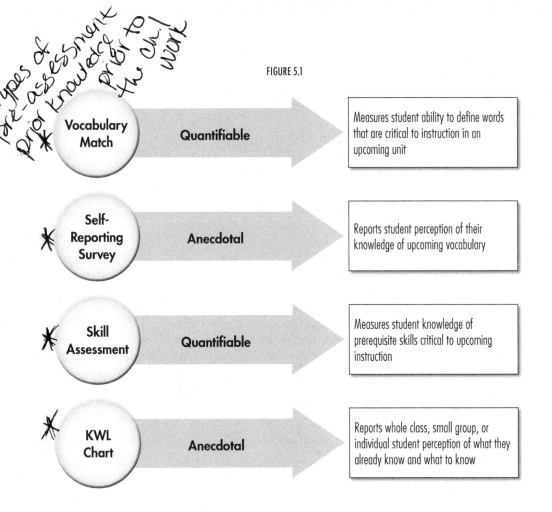

Vocabulary Match	Quantifiable	Measures student ability to define words that are critical to instruction in an upcoming unit
Self-Reporting Survey	Anecdotal	Reports student perception of their knowledge of upcoming vocabulary
Skill Assessment	Quantifiable	Measures student knowledge of prerequisite skills critical to upcoming instruction
KWL Chart	Anecdotal	Reports whole class, small group, or individual student perception of what they already know and what to know

Pre-assessment tools require careful alignment between the content of the assessment and the instruction to come. The following four examples illustrate some options for determining prior knowledge for a language arts unit focused on types of reading comprehension and writing.

- **Vocabulary Matching**: Matching of key vocabulary terms tied to major concepts in the unit provides us with insight into students' familiarity with upcoming concepts. This pre-assessment approach consists of matching terms and definitions or examples. The results of vocabulary matching are quantifiable and can be used at most grade levels and with most subjects.

TABLE 5.1

#	Term	Answer	#	Definition
1	Narrative		a	Composition whose purpose is to move a reader by argument or entreaty to a belief, position, or course of action
2	Persuasive		b	A story or narrated account of actual or fictional events
3	Exposition		c	A composition whose purpose is to set forth or explain

- **Self-Report**: In this pre-assessment strategy, students report on their own depth of word knowledge. Teachers can use this anecdotal feedback as a starting point to plan initial instruction surrounding a concept. Figure 5.2, adapted from Paribakht and Wesche, 1997, illustrates a self –report that can also be used for most grade levels and most subject areas.

Can rate their level of knowledge / familar

TABLE 5.2

Vocabulary Terms	Never saw it before	Heard it but don't know the meaning	Recognize it in context as having something to do with	Can use the word in a sentence
Persuasion			✓	
Exposition		✓		
Narrative				✓

- **Skill assessments**: Skill assessments are used to determine if students have the pre-requisite knowledge necessary to hook previous learning onto new skills. The skills we are looking for in such an assessment are those skills upon which new learning depends.

TABLE 5.3

Should Know How to	To Learn to
Identify the main idea	Identify supporting details
Defend an argument	Write a persuasive essay
Use transition words	Write a narrative

- **KWL Chart**: The teacher lists terms, concepts, and skills in the KWL. Students write about what they already know and want to know. The final column, "What did I learn?" can be used at the end of instruction of each concept or lesson as wrap up. The chart below is an example of use for both skill and vocabulary in a KWL chart.

TABLE 5.4

Term or Concept	What do I know?	What do I Want to Know?	What did I learn?
Point of View			
Finding the main idea			

These four types of pre-assessment inform us about the student's prior knowledge before beginning a unit or chapter. Do students have the background knowledge to fully grasp the instruction that will come, or do they need some pre-teaching/frontloading to help them make connections from the known (prior knowledge) to the unknown (the subject matter that is coming)?

How Do the Data Inform Instruction?

Assembling the information from pre-assessments leads back to the unit plan. Based on the pattern of student responses, teachers can, if needed, adjust the original plan to develop students' background knowledge and adjust the rate of gradual release in response to the results.

FIGURE 5.2

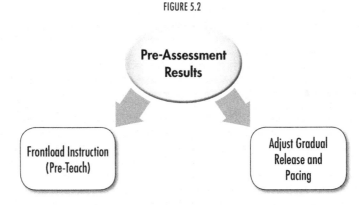

Frontload Instruction

If pre-assessment indicates a low level of key concept background knowledge, skill application, and terminology, then adjust the lesson plan and pace to allow for pre-teaching. Frontloading instruction helps students develop familiarity with vocabulary terms and concepts before actual instruction begins. It also allows the teacher time to tie new concepts to the students' lives and prior knowledge.

Patterns of pre-assessment performance determine the group structure for frontloading. We want the students to have enough prior knowledge so that we can "hook" that knowledge to upcoming instruction. The following graphic provides some options for grouping in order to frontload necessary concept or vocabulary prior to teaching a lesson.

FIGURE 5.3

Whole Class "No Hook"	• Most or all students lack any background knowledge. • Frontload important vocabulary and background knowledge for the whole class.
Small Group "Some Hook"	• Pattern of background knowledge varies. • Frontload for small groups or use peer tutoring
Move Forward "Big Hook"	• Most or all students have background knowledge necessary to understand upcoming instruction. • Move forward with your original lesson plan and address the needs of the few in small groups after the lesson.

In addition to the decision to pre-teach or not, teachers have options about how to deliver the necessary Tier 1 prerequisite skills and concepts that are not already being taught in Tier 2 or Tier 3. Responding to student need is not always clear-cut. Rather, instruction can seem messy when we are responding to the variety of needs of the students in front of us. The following two scenarios depict student pre-assessment results and a teacher's options for providing the background knowledge for success.

Classroom Scenario 1: A 9th grade class tally of two literary terms in the table below indicates that all students will benefit from some pre-teaching. Because none of the students report knowledge of either term, whole class pre-teaching will help everyone to develop the hook they need to absorb new information. Students with below-grade level comprehension skills will need small group reinforcement with supplementary materials in addition to whole group instruction.

[handwritten: – whole class]
[handwritten: – below level small group addtl.]

TABLE 5.5

Vocabulary Terms	Never saw it before	Heard it but don't know the meaning	Recognize it in context as having something to do with …	Can use the word in a sentence
Persuasion	8	20		
Inference	18	10		

Classroom Scenario 2: Conversely, the next chart below shows the same class with different results. This is a more typical result in a diverse Tier 1 class. In this case, we see that up to 19 students are unfamiliar with the vocabulary terms while 16 students recognize the words or can use them in a sentence. However, a clear majority of the class has at least heard the words. Now the teacher has three choices:

- Pre-teach all students to provide background for some, reinforcement and review for others.

- Convene carefully structured small groups before instruction to provide background for some and extension for others.

- Move forward with instruction, and plan for reinforcement and re-teaching for some students during small group instruction.

Ex. front loading (handwritten annotation)

TABLE 5.6

Vocabulary Terms	Never saw it before	Heard it but don't know the meaning	Recognize it in context as having something to do with ...	Can use the word in a sentence
Persuasion	6	13	5	3
Inference	5	7	14	2

Whatever choice a teacher makes relative to frontloading, it is effective practice to determine the knowledge base of our students. Frontloading, when indicated by pre-assessments, entails using a small amount of focused time now rather than spending copious amounts of time later to fill in the gaps.

Practical Application: To Frontload or Not to Frontload

Use the pre-assessment data for a 6th grade class on the chart below to make the following decisions Use the questions and previous examples as a guide. Answers will vary.

- Will you frontload all or some of the following vocabulary terms? If so, which terms and how will you accomplish this? Will you provide:

    1. Whole class frontloading for all terms?

    2. A combination of whole class and small group frontloading?

    3. Move forward and convene small re-teaching groups after instruction?

    4. What enrichment will you provide during frontloading for students who already know the terms?

Vocabulary Terms	Never saw it before	Heard it but don't know the meaning.	Recognize it in context as having something to do with	Can use the word in a sentence
Simile	6	13	5	3
Metaphor	5	7	14	1
Analogy	10	12	5	

Whole class small group =Both

Gradual Release of Responsibility

As discussed in Chapter 2, gradual release of responsibility relates directly to the level of students' knowledge and skills. The extent to which students have learned the latter helps us decide if we need to accelerate our pace or slow it down to allow for additional modeling and guided practice. The more modeling and practice needed, the slower the pace and vice versa.

TABLE 5.7

Pre-Assessment Affects Gradual Release

If Pre-Assessment indicates	Then adjust gradual release of responsibility by
Students' prior knowledge is limited across a class	**Slowing the pace of gradual release of responsibility** • Teach smaller chunks of information • More explicit modeling • More explicit guided practice • Slow the pace of instruction • Provide extension activities or increased pace for students with strong knowledge of upcoming concepts
Students' prior knowledge is varied across a class	**Moderating the pace of gradual release of responsibility** • Model and provide guided practice before releasing students for independent practice. • Convene small groups for those who do not have prior knowledge to provide more modeling and guided practice
Students have a strong familiarity with upcoming concepts.	**Accelerating gradual release of responsibility** • Increase the pace of instruction for the whole class • Modeling and practice for student success during independent practice. • Allow time in small groups for reinforcement for students in need

Classroom Scenario: Mr. Jones is going to teach students to identify supporting details in an informational reading selection. In order to determine the students' prior knowledge, he gives the students a passage and asks them to identify the main idea. The skill assessment depicted in the chart below shows the results for Mr. Jones's class. Eight students have successfully identified the main idea while eighteen students were unable to do so. These results tell Mr. Jones that his instruction, in addition to frontloading, will require substantial modeling and guided practice for most of his class before releasing students for independent work. Mr. Jones alters his original lesson plan because he knows that the slower pace will meet the needs of his students. These results also show Mr. Jones that if the eight students who have the pre-requisite skill progress at a faster rate, he will have to provide opportunities for them to develop deeper, more sophisticated understanding and application of the skill with enrichment activities in grade level or supplementary text.

TABLE 5.8

Skill Assessment	Ready	Not Ready
Find the main idea in an informational passage	8	18

Gradual release of responsibility is like a dance. We adjust our steps and pace according to student need, providing more or less modeling and guided practice. As teachers, we know that every class, every year, is different, with varied needs and rates of learning. While this process begins with pre-assessment, it continues throughout our instruction in response to the students in front of us and should become a natural part of the instructional process.

Practical Application: Gradual Release of Responsibility

A new unit for 5th grade requires students to learn to write a persuasive essay. The teacher knows that students should have learned to defend an argument in the previous grade. To gauge the class's prior knowledge, the teacher asks students to defend the argument that texting should be allowed in class.

Use the results from the table below to predict how slowly or quickly the teacher can release responsibility for learning to the students. Although answers will vary, discuss this scenario with your colleagues to come to consensus.

1. How much explicit modeling and guided practice will students need for each of the skills below? Remember that the need for explicit instruction increases with the degree of instructional challenge for students.

2. Your original plan was to spend one week on the new skill. Based on the student report, how will your pace change?

3. Will you accomplish the adjustments in gradual release in a whole class or small group setting?

4. What activities will you provide in small group work to meet the varied needs of your students?

New Skill	Prerequisite Skill Assessment	Ready	Not Ready
Write a persuasive essay	Write a paragraph to defend the argument that students should be allow to use texting in class	15	12

Pre-assessment provides an additional layer of information that helps us refine our lesson plans to meet the needs of our students. Due to its informal nature, pre-assessment is not usually included in the bigger arena of assessment. However, a little adjustment at the beginning of a unit or chapter can go a long way to helping us deliver more effective and efficient instruction.

CHAPTER SIX

During Instruction

During Instruction: Responding to Student Performance

In Chapter 5, we outlined the necessity of using various forms of pre-assessment to help teachers shape their lessons and judge how quickly or slowly their students can use new information or skills independently. However, our response to data does not end with pre-assessment. In the course of teaching a lesson, every action and reaction from students provide ongoing data that affects our instruction and their learning. Student response to instruction causes us to pivot or change direction, sometimes mid-lesson. Even the best planned lessons sometimes go awry. Rather than trudging through lessons that are clearly not working, we can change direction in response to the data we gather during the act of teaching.

Data Source: Formative Assessment

All data inform instruction. As discussed in Chapter 4, however, formative assessment is unique in that it occurs during instruction rather than before or after instruction. Heritage, 2010 states: *"Only by keeping a very close eye on emerging learning through formative assessment can teachers be prospective, determining what is within the students' reach, and providing them with experiences to support and extend learning* (pg. 8)." Formative assessment is both informal and semi-formal and allows us to analyze student learning as it evolves. Informal assessments include student behavioral responses, verbal answers, and non-graded daily class-work, while semi-formal assessment includes graded curriculum-based assignments, activities, as well as quizzes and tests administered at various times during instruction. A teacher's response to formative assessment data is at the heart of effective Tier 1 instruction.

Although many types of formative assessment are available to teachers, we have chosen three types of data most commonly used during Tier 1 instruction in order to illustrate the causal effect of data on instruction:

FIGURE 6.1

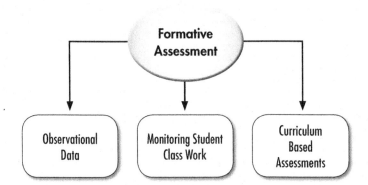

- **Observational Data**

  - Awareness of student behavioral response to instruction. The two most frequently observable behaviors are:
    - Participation
    - On-task behavior
  - Observational data, based on student behavior, informs us about the students' response to instruction. It is usually the first piece of data available once we begin teaching. On-task behavior and participation is an "in the moment" indicator of successful instruction and subsequent learning.

- **Monitoring Student Work**

  - Constant review of student class work (both oral and written) to determine if students understand the instruction and are able to demonstrate their learning in class work
  - Monitoring students' work tells us about student errors and misunderstandings as they grapple with new learning.

- **Curriculum-Based Assessments (CBA)**

  - Criterion-referenced quizzes and tests developed by teachers or publishers and designed to determine students' learning at regular intervals during the instructional process of a lesson, chapter, or unit.

i.e. end of chapter

How Do Formative Assessments Inform Instruction?

Formative assessment provides the opportunity to improve our practice in three ways: fostering/stimulating student engagement, providing feedback, and grouping to re-teach, reinforce, and enrich. Although they overlap, each type of data can be tied to a specific teacher response as illustrated in the graphic below.

FIGURE 6.2

Teacher Response to Formative Assessment

Observational Data	Increase engagement	*Student engagement*
Monitoring Student Work	Provide feedback and adjust instruction	*adjustment while teaching*
Curriculum Based Assessment	Reteach, reinforce, enrich	*reteach Did the learn the skill?*

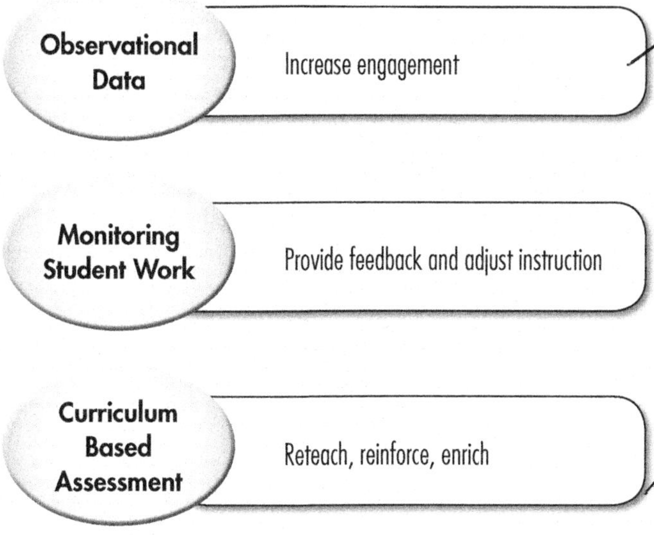

When teachers pay attention to students' responses to instruction, it leads to changes that result in improved learning and engagement. The end of the chapter or unit is too late to find out if students are internalizing and generalizing the information and skills being taught. Let's delve into these responses to formative assessment.

Observational Data to Increase Engagement

We engage students in two ways: (1) using strategies that are designed to elicit response and participation from all students; and (2) designing instruction and tasks that pique student interest and challenge students to expand their learning. While teaching, we observe students who are off-task and not participating. They have their heads on the desk, or they are texting, talking, and daydreaming. Sometimes students may not participate and appear bored because they are frustrated during the lesson and activities. Other students appear bored simply because the work is too easy or they choose not to participate, even if they have the opportunity. Whatever the reason, off-task behavior requires immediate action. It is an indication that we need to change direction. In order to accomplish this, we must quickly analyze why students might be off-task or not participating and then adjust our instruction to engage them.

Historical and pre-assessment data helps teachers determine what students already know and are able to do. It is part of cognitive preparation for instruction and continues to inform our practice as we deliver instruction and gauge student response. Clearly, the more we know about our students and the possible challenges of the work, the more likely we are to quickly ascertain the reason for student disengagement. The decision to pivot, that is change direction to engage students, is not complicated. The best responses during instruction are usually immediate and simple.

Engagement strategies are many and varied. Which one the teacher selects at any given moment depends directly on her analysis of a student's off-task behavior. The following examples illustrate types of responses to student disengagement.

FIGURE 6.3

Observation	Possible Cause	Response
Students quickly finish assignments and appear bored.	Task is too easy	Increase the pace of instruction/provide more challenging tasks
Only three students raise their hands to answer questions	Low level expectation of being called on	Use random selection of students to answer questions using sticks/cards
Students do not participate or complete work	Task is too difficult	Slow the pace, provide more modeling and practice using supplementary materials
Students do not participate and appear confused	Lack of prior knowledge or different cultural experiences	Provide an example that relates instruction to students' lives and culture

In addition to the previous examples, partner work and choral repetition and response are strategies that engage students regardless of the cause of non-participation. Partner work provides opportunities for students to work together for various amounts of time for different purposes. This strategy provides processing time, increases the level of student-to-student academic talk, and develops higher-level problem solving skills. Partner work can take place in as little as a minute for quick processing or as long as a class period for problem solving or partner writing—and any amount of time in between.

Advanced students can work with partners of like ability or become peer tutors. Struggling students are more likely to engage if they have someone to work with. English learners benefit from having partners with the same first language who can explain concepts as they work. Additionally, working with a peer elicits a heightened level of personal accountability. Figure 6.4 below illustrates some simple partner activities for varied amounts of time. Using partner work efficiently breaks up instruction into more manageable chunks and allows for the processing time that is so critical if we expect students to internalize and generalize information.

FIGURE 6.4

Partner Work

2 minutes	5 minutes	10 minutes	30 minutes
Compare answers	Identify the most important information	Identify author's position with citations	Research a topic on the internet with notes and citations
Tell your partner why you think your answer is correct.	Share opinions	Partner reading	Begin a draft of a research paper

Choral response and repetition are strategies that increase participation and/or provide additional practice. Purposeful choral response and repetition ensure that all students are getting repeated exposures to important information. Although teachers use choral response and repetition more frequently in elementary school, it is just as effective in middle and high school. Students' need for extra practice does not diminish when students grow taller. The following two examples illustrate the difference between purposeless and purposeful choral repetition.

The example in Figure 6.5 illustrates choral repetition and response without purpose. Notice that the teacher simply asks the students to repeat the word *narrative*. Since the students do not connect the word to the definition, they do not achieve deeper understanding or internalize the term. They only know how to pronounce the word.

FIGURE 6.5

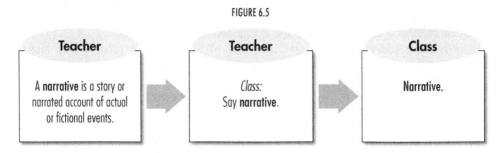

Let's contrast this with the following example where choral repetition has a purpose. Notice that the teacher asks the class to respond with the entire definition of the word *narrative*, using a complete sentence. This ensures that the students are practicing the whole definition, provides additional practice, and encourages participation.

FIGURE 6.6

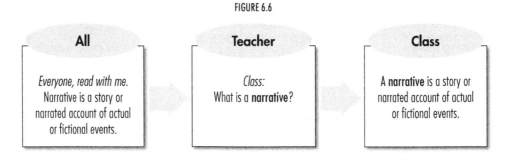

Clearly, the use of choral response and repetition must be selective and purposeful. A class full of chanting students will not result in deeper understanding of complex concepts, but it will help students retain important definitions, facts, and procedures.

Whatever the reason for off-task behavior and non-participation, students must be re-engaged in tasks and participate in the lesson in order to learn. It is up to teachers to use observational data determine the reason for disengagement and to respond in a way that encourages students to fully participate in their learning.

Practical Application: Engage Students in Their Own Learning

You are teaching a unit on writing research papers. While discussing and teaching the importance of citations, you notice that half the class has checked out. How would you engage students in this rather dry topic? Use the checklist below to identify which strategies you would use and then explain how you would adjust instruction to incorporate those strategies.

Strategy	Check If Yes	Detail Your Response
Increase the pace and provide more challenging examples?		
Use random selection of students to answer questions?		
Slow the pace and provide more modeling and practice?		
Relate the examples to student interest, lives, and/or culture?		
Use partner work to practice examples?		
Use choral repetition and response to make sure students understand the rules for citations?		
Other: Explain		

Monitoring Student Work to Target Feedback

Providing immediate feedback to students is perhaps the most effective use of formative assessment. Targeted feedback improves learning while it is happening (Heritage, 2010). Feedback is usually descriptive and helps students recognize their errors or misconceptions. Teachers provide feedback in response to an oral error or after observing a number of errors during class-work. Teachers offer feedback in various ways, depending on the nature of the mistake or misconception.

For example, if the error involves a discrete skill such as a student's mispronunciation or misspelling, the teacher provides feedback relevant to that mistake by modeling correct pronunciation while echoing the student's answer. However, if a student or group of students demonstrates misunderstanding of more complex skills and concepts, the teacher adjusts instruction to provide feedback for one or all students through additional modeling and practice with a focus on clarifying patterns of errors. In either case, teachers should never publicly single out a student or use a technique that will embarrass a student. For example, if a student makes a word pronunciation error, we restate the answer and ask for repetition from the whole class, not just a single student. Additionally, techniques such as "phone a friend" or check with a neighbor provides feedback and can help a struggling student be more successful and thus more likely to participate. The following scenarios provide options for feedback based on student errors or misconceptions. We begin with an example of appropriate and inappropriate reaction to student mistakes.

Example/Non-example of effective feedback—Students are assigned to write a paragraph in two different classes. At the end of the day, each teacher reviews the paragraphs and discovers that the majority of students are omitting commas to set off a beginning phrase or clause. Although the teachers have already taught that skill, it seems that the students are unable to generalize the information when they are writing independently.

FIGURE 6.7

Feedback

Example of incorrect feedback
- The teacher corrects each paper, inserts red commas in the appropriate places, and returns the papers the next day.
- No additional instruction is provided.

Example of correct feedback
- The teacher corrects each paper but does not insert commas.
- The next day, the teacher reteaches the use of commas to set off introductory phrases and clauses. She then asks students to re-read their paragraphs and insert commas in the appropriate places while she monitors the class.

In the example above, notice that the first teacher simply corrects the errors but does not alter her instruction based on the pattern of errors. We can be certain that most of the students who received the red commas have no idea why they were incorrect and will continue to make the same mistake. However, the second teacher—while exasperated that she has already taught this skill---recognizes that the students need a description of the error and re-teaching. Self-correcting will provide necessary additional practice.

Classroom samples: The following samples depict various classroom scenarios and include one or more options for teachers to provide appropriate descriptive feedback.

- **Sample 1**: A student answers an oral question and makes a subject/verb agreement error. The teacher wants to address that error not only for that student but also for others who make the same mistake. He immediately provides feedback for the student in the context of the whole class.

FIGURE 6.8

Feedback through restatement

- Teacher restates the answer with correct subject/verb agreement and asks the class to repeat the answer. The teacher explains why the form is correct.
- Teacher asks another question, models correct subject verb agreement, and asks the class to repeat.
- Teacher gives students a sentence stem and requires a response that demonstrates subject/verb agreement.

- **Sample 2**: A teacher has just taught the development of a thesis statement in an introductory paragraph. He is walking around the room and finds that many students are having difficulty developing their statements. After three students ask the same question, it is apparent that this problem is not an isolated one. The teacher determines that the students need immediate feedback. He considers her options for providing feedback.

FIGURE 6.9

Feedback for individual students

- Teacher moves from student to student to provide individual feedback on how to develop a thesis statement.

Feedback through peer tutoring

- Teacher pairs students who understand how to develop a thesis statement with those who do not. Peer tutors assist the students having difficulty while the teacher observes.

Feedback with whole class and small group

- Teacher reconvenes the class and provides additional models and practice with thesis statements and then works in a small group with the students who are having difficulty.

- **Sample 3**: Students are learning to write a narrative essay. As the teacher monitors student work, he discovers that many of the students are using the words "*And then*" as transitions to sequence events. The teacher realizes that he assumed that the students would already know and be able to use appropriate transition words when writing the paragraph. He also knows that this cannot be left uncorrected. The teacher considers the following options to adjust his instruction to include the teaching or re-teaching of transition words.

FIGURE 6.10

Feedback for individual students	• The teacher moves from student to student to teach transition words to those who need it and lets the lesson progress. As a result, the teacher spends the entire lesson teaching transition words to each individual student.
Feedback through a mini lesson	• The teacher conducts an informal survey to see how many students understand the use of transition words. • If a pattern exists across the class, the teacher stops the lesson to teach a mini-lesson on appropriate transition words.
Feedback at another time during instruction	• The teacher notes the misunderstanding and lets the students continue but plans to specifically address transition words during the revision process.

The previous examples provide options for feedback, but the most important point in this section is that constant monitoring of student work and timely feedback is essential if we are to ensure that students are not only learning but internalizing the skills and concepts that we teach. Failure to monitor ongoing student work results in less than optimum student performance on quizzes, tests, and external measures. *Basically, we either monitor work during instruction or students and teachers suffer for it later.*

Practical Application: Structuring Feedback

Based on the following data collected while monitoring student work, how would you structure feedback to improve students' understanding of similes and metaphors?

Scenario: This week's instructional focus was on similes and metaphors. You first introduced similes and provided practice, then taught metaphors and again provided practice. Everyone seemed to understand until they had to work through various examples and identify both similes and metaphors. Your observation revealed that the students could not discriminate between the two when working with text. Use the previous examples and explanations to determine the best course of action for you class. Include additional options that you have used successfully in the past. Do you …

Feedback Strategy	Yes or No	Detail Your Feedback Structure
Restate the definition of each and let students progress through the selection?		
Move from student to student to explain the difference?		
Let the students continue the work, correct it, and plan to re-teach the next day?		
Stop the activity and re-teach both literary devices using examples to show contrast and practice with the students before allowing them to proceed?		
Other: Explain		

Grouping to Re-Teach, Reinforce, and Enrich Based on CBA

Curriculum-based assessment data (quizzes, graded assignments, and tests) as well as other forms of formative assessment collected during instruction informs us of the need to re-teach, reinforce, and/or enrich. If all students are performing at proficient levels, we simply move to the next concept/unit. In a diverse Tier 1 class, this is rarely the case. It is more likely that we will encounter a variety of results. When considering our response to student performance on assessments, we must first reflect on the validity of the assessment itself, as discussed in Chapter 2:

- Did the assessment reflect the format, content, and language of the tasks during instruction and vice versa?
- Did we include assessment items that reflected the hierarchy of *must know, should know, could know* levels of standard acquisition?
- Did we provide assessments that reflected the language skills of students already receiving intervention?

If the answer to the questions above is no, then, in addition to working with students, we must revise our future instructional tasks and/or assessments so that the task predicts the performance on curriculum based assessments and any external measures that students will take in the future. However, if the answer to the questions above is yes, then we begin the process of addressing the actual results of the assessment.

Additionally, our initial planning for levels of standard acquisition (*must know, should know,* or *could know*) now assumes a more specific role. Before we group to re-teach, reinforce, and enrich, we must think about the skills that students brought to the initial instruction and first determine if they met their goals.

- Were all students proficient on the *must know, should know* and *could know* levels of standard acquisition at their functioning literacy level?
- How many students scored proficient or close to proficient on the *should know* level using grade level text? How many should have scored proficient?
- How many students were able to demonstrate knowledge at the *could know* level?

Based on analysis of the data and student goals, we begin the process of specific grouping to re-teach, reinforce, and enrich. Although these groups focus primarily on students who did not perform at expected levels, we must also provide rigorous work, rather than busy work, for students who demonstrated proficiency. The purpose of grouping is to target instruction based on the data and bring the students toward more proficient or advanced achievement. The re-teach and reinforce groups require teacher-delivered explicit instruction while the enrichment group can often work independently to deepen their knowledge of the instructional objectives.

FIGURE 6.11

Reteach for Students Who Are Not Proficient	Reinforce for Students Who Are Barely Proficient	Enrich for Students Who Are Already Proficient
• Supplementary and/or grade level materials • Modeling and practice with a different approach	• Grade level materials • Provide additional modeling and practice on targeted concepts and skills	• Advanced supplementary and grade level materials • Deepen concept/skill knowledge through investigation and analysis

Let's get a little more specific. The following example shows the results of a short quiz on unit vocabulary and the teacher's response to the results.

TABLE 6.1

Student Name	Quiz #1: Vocabulary
Student #1	80% (tion)
Student #2	70% (tion)
Student #3	40% (tion)
Student #4	30% (tion)
Student #5	65%
Student #6	100%

While reviewing the quiz, the teacher sees that student results are varied. In addition, the teacher notices that the four of the six students spelled the suffix "tion" as "shun". The teacher decides to spend some time the next day in small feedback groups to re-teach and reinforce the unit vocabulary. However, before breaking into groups, the teacher decides to review the correct spelling and meaning of the suffix "tion" for the entire class. Although this spelling pattern is not the focus of the quiz, the teacher realizes that this error is occurring across most of his class and must be addressed. The teacher's grouping strategy is illustrated below.

FIGURE 6.12

RETEACH Students #3 and #4	REINFORCE Students #2 and #5	ENRICH Students #1 and #6
• Reteach and practice vocabulary both orally and in writing. Make sure students can read the words in context. Students work with partners to practice the words. Use supplementary materials as needed.	• Review the words in the context of grade level texts. Students work with partners to define the vocabulary in their own words and write sentences using the vocabulary.	• Ask students to identify synonyms for the vocabulary that fit into the context of grade level material and more difficult text and explain their reasoning for choosing a specific synonym.

Formative assessment is the means by which we determine which students are learning and to what extent. The data the teacher collects during instruction provides insight into who is learning and who is not. However, data review alone is not enough to change the course of student progress. The parameters of Tier 1 require that teachers respond to formative assessment immediately and effectively to guarantee student progress.

Practical Application: Grouping Students Based on Formative Assessment

Use the following data set to determine how and if you will group students to re-teach, reinforce, and enrich. The purpose of the activity is to analyze your current instructional response to formative assessment and to use the previous information as a guide to continue, adjust, or expand your future practice. Explain your reasoning and the instruction for each group.

Quiz #8: Identifying Supporting Details—Student Results

Student	Percent Correct	Student	Percent Correct
James	40%	Raul	65%
Marissa	90%	Michael	85%
Juan	60%	Monserat	40%
Sochi	85%	Peter	70%
Maria	100%	Margaret	20%
Frances	70%	Yadhira	75%

List the student names in the appropriate column and describe the instruction you will use for each group.

RE-TEACH	REINFORCE	ENRICH
Method used:	Method used:	Method used:

Beyond the Threshold of Tier 1?

— Does the data exdie a need for addtl skill dev. Tier II?

The role of formative assessment in Tier 1 instruction is to ensure students are moving forward to proficient and advanced levels of performance. However, formative assessment in the Tier 1 classroom serves another purpose: it helps to identify students who may have reached the threshold of Tier 1. An integral part of RtI is the identification of students who may benefit from additional skill development beyond the scope of Tier 1.

The four-point rule is one way to determine if students may have reached this threshold and require further investigation to determine specific needs that might be met in Tiers 2 or 3. This rule, as described in Chapter 3, helps us to track student progress over time relative to a targeted level of performance. The following two examples illustrate how to use the four-point rule on a line graph, in a grade book, and a rubric over approximately 6-8 weeks of instruction.

Example 1: XYZ school district has determined that 75% on Tier 1 formative assessments is the indicator that students are meeting expectations. The results of graded assignments, quizzes, and tests for a 7th grade student documented below show that the student began the year above grade level. However, as instruction progressed, the student began to perform below proficient levels. Short-term differentiation and re-teaching was not enough to bring the student back to proficient levels of performance. Once the student performed below proficient levels on four consecutive assignments, quizzes and tests, she was referred to the RtI team for further investigation and assessment.

TABLE 6.2

7th grade Student
Grade-Book Example—Expected Percentage 75%

Quiz #1	Test #1	Quiz#2	Test #2	Quiz #2	Test#3	Quiz#4
80%	85%	75%	70%	40%	60%	50%

Bar graph display of the same data.

FIGURE 6.13

Student Performance

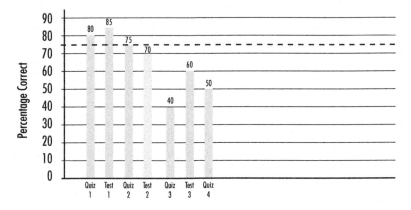

Example 2: In contrast, the data for another 7th grade student depicted below demonstrates that the student began to slip at the third data point. However, short-term differentiation for this student ameliorated the problem and the student returned to proficient status. In this case, the student would not be referred to the RtI team but would continue to receive differentiated instruction and close monitoring.

TABLE 6.3

Grade Book Example

Quiz #1	Test #1	Quiz #2	Test #2	Quiz#3	Test #3
75%	80%	70%	55%	70%	85%

Bar graph display of the same data.

FIGURE 6.14

Student Performance

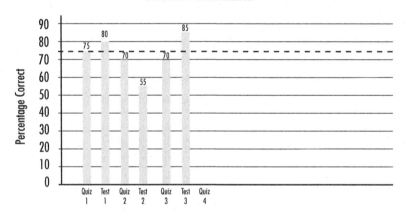

In addition to grade books and line graphs, many schools use rubrics to rate student work. Rubrics, which allow teachers to establish criteria for performance, provide an additional form of data to use in the four point rule. In Chapter 1, we referenced Marzano and Kendall's New Taxonomy (2008) as a way to guide the development of tasks. The developers of the taxonomy advocate the use of rubrics to determine students' depth of understanding and application of skills. Since rubrics can be customized by grade level, subject, and task, they are flexible and adaptable based on targeted areas of performance. Rubrics guide teachers to develop tasks and determine the degree to which students are able to demonstrate their learning using a scale of ".5" (weak performance) to "4.0" (strong performance). For example, a rating of "1.0" alerts the teacher that a student was able to complete a task "With help, a partial understanding of some of the the simpler details and proccesses but not the more complex ideas and processes (pg.169)." Alternatively, a rating of "3" tells the teacher that the student performed the task with "No major errors or omissions regarding any of the information and/or processes (simple or complex) that were explicitly taught." Adoption of a school-wide scoring rubric for Tier 1 tasks and assessments promotes consistency within and across grades and provides a criteria-based description of student performance in addition to percentages or letter grades. Whether a rubric is publisher, district, or school developed, teachers can use the instrument in conjunction with the four point rule to determine if a student is at risk in Tier 1.

Whatever method teachers use to evaluate students' learning, data from quizzes and tests alone are not enough to refer a student to the RtI team. If the student has not responded to Tier 1 instruction as evidenced by formative curriculum-based assessments and has been provided with short-term differentiation, the teacher should be concerned. If the student *continually* requires differentiation similar to what students are receiving in Tier 2 or Tier 3 interventions, then the student's name should be referred to the RtI team as a possible candidate for services beyond the Tier 1 classroom. Figure 6.15 below illustrates the progression of events necessary to refer a student to the RtI team.

FIGURE 6.15

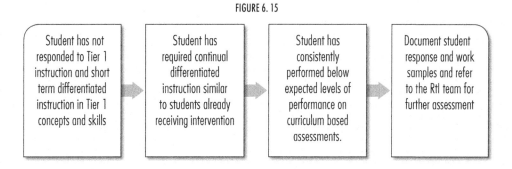

Referring a student to intervention must be timely and warranted. We don't want the student to languish in a classroom in which he or she cannot succeed. However, we don't want Tier 2 intervention to become a dumping ground for every student who might be experiencing a temporary problem in Tier 1. Before referral to intervention, teachers must attempt research-based Tier 1 interventions and differentiation to ameliorate the problem. Intervention is not just more of the core. At the risk of redundancy, we must consider the results of formative assessment in combination with the duration and type of differentiation when making the decision to refer a student to the RtI Team.

CHAPTER SEVEN

After Instruction

Formative assessments help us improve instruction *during* a lesson or series of lessons. Summative assessments tell us what our students have learned at the end of major units of instruction. Summative assessment differs from formative assessment in that summative assessment is considered an assessment *of* learning rather than an assessment *for* learning (Buffum, et al 2009). Both are critical in a strong Tier 1 curriculum and part of the larger cycle of instruction and intervention.

Data Source: Summative Assessments

Summative assessments are administered at specific points in time to determine student learning at the end of an instructional unit. As discussed in Chapter 3, teachers usually administer these assessments after a chapter, unit, or course of study. Summative assessments also include external measures such as periodic standards-based assessments and yearly state or national assessments. In these instances, assessment occurs at a specific pre-determined point in time to measure student acquisition of grade level standards. Summative assessments play a role in predicting students' performance on subsequent high stakes tests.

Figure 7.1 below illustrates the relationship of each type of summative assessment. The smaller gear (end of chapter, unit, or course) forecasts student performance on the larger gear. Periodic standards-based assessments, in turn, drive student performance on the largest gear—the yearly state or national standards based assessments. The level of prediction is, of course, dependent on the degree to which in-class summative assessments reflect the tasks included in the external measures.

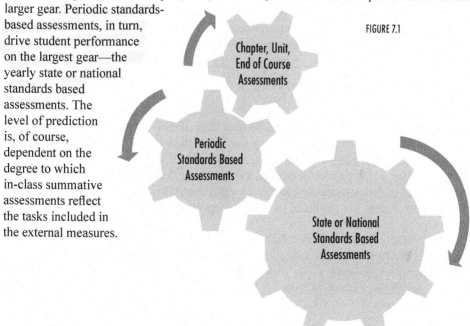

FIGURE 7.1

Chapter, Unit, End of Course Assessments

Periodic Standards Based Assessments

State or National Standards Based Assessments

Summative assessments help determine to what extent students have internalized and can generalize Tier 1 standards-based concepts and skills taught over a specific period of time. Each type of summative assessment, whether classroom-based or an external measure, provides specific information about student learning as illustrated in Figure 7.2.

FIGURE 7.2

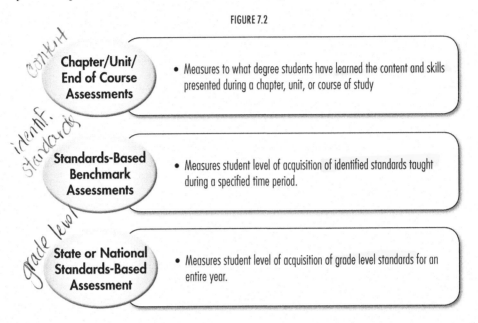

Although reading screens are not typically considered summative assessments, we have included reading screens at this juncture in the assessment cycle. As we discussed in Chapter 3, sometimes assessment tools are used for non-traditional purposes. In an RtI system, many schools use a reading comprehension measure in grades 3-12 as part of their quarter or trimester assessment schedule to determine student growth in comprehension. Ideally, the results of a reading comprehension screen should correlate with student performance on more traditional summative assessments. In these cases, we can say that reading assessments are used summatively.

How Do the Data Inform Instruction?

Summative assessment offers the opportunity to measure student progress by comparing current results to those of previous summative instruments. This in turn helps us reflect on the effectiveness of our past planning and instruction and at the same time provides information for the future. One way to use summative assessments is to reconfigure our class RtI triangle. Summative data helps us identify students who (1) may have reached the threshold of Tier 1 instruction and thus need additional service; and (2) may no longer require intervention. The results of the assessments may change the percentage of students in each tier.

Additionally, student performance on these measures assists in shaping future instruction. Patterns of performance lend insight regarding student readiness for the next installment of instruction. These patterns can result in instructional revision based on student success or challenge. Figure 7.3 below describes two ways summative assessment informs instruction.

FIGURE 7.3

Revise Your Triangle

- Are more students performing at Tier 1 levels than when we started instruction?
- Are any additional students candidates for referral to the RtI team?
- Are any students already receiving intervention performing at proficient levels?

Reflect on Your Instruction to Move Forward

- Did my instruction reflect the tasks of the external measures?
- What should I have done differently to push more students to proficient and advanced?
- What are my students' strengths and weaknesses?
- What will I change in my future instruction?

Revise Your RtI Triangle

In Chapter 4, we met Ms. Young who developed her beginning classroom RtI triangle based on data derived from the previous year's assessments. She found that her initial triangle configuration included 33% of students proficient in Tier 1, 38% eligible for Tier 2 services, and 28% that may have needed tier 3 services. This configuration was far from the optimum proportion of 80–15–5. She used the information to plan and differentiate instruction, and to choose supplementary materials for the upcoming year. Ms. Young's original triangle is depicted below.

FIGURE 7.4

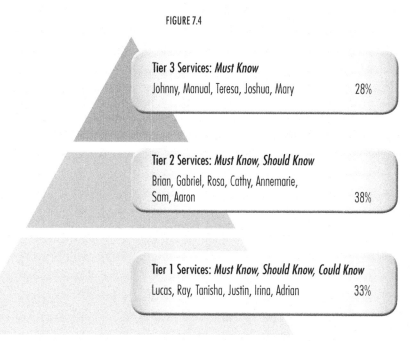

Tier 3 Services: *Must Know*
Johnny, Manual, Teresa, Joshua, Mary   28%

Tier 2 Services: *Must Know, Should Know*
Brian, Gabriel, Rosa, Cathy, Annemarie, Sam, Aaron   38%

Tier 1 Services: *Must Know, Should Know, Could Know*
Lucas, Ray, Tanisha, Justin, Irina, Adrian   33%

Kukic (2009), in his discussion of RtI, suggests that schools and teachers use the optimum triangle configuration of 80-15-5 as a goal to determine if instruction is moving the class toward the optimum configuration in Tier 1. Accordingly, at the end of the first trimester, Ms. Young again analyzed her data and revisited her triangle to assess possible tier changes. The number of students in Tier 1 had increased, but so had the number of students who appeared to require Tier 3 intervention. Using the results of standards-based benchmark exams and a reading screen, Ms. Young revised her triangle configuration to reflect the new proportions of 44-22-33. Ms. Young's new triangle is illustrated below. It shows that Ms. Young's class is moving closer to the goal for Tier 1, but the increased percentage of students in Tier 3 intervention requires more analysis.

FIGURE 7.5

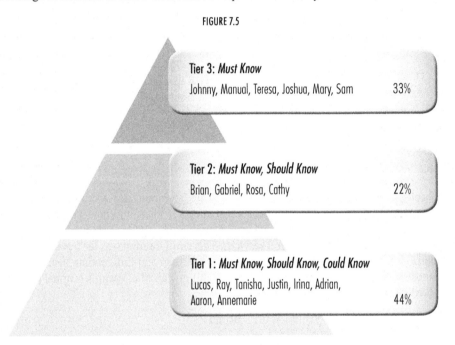

Tier 3: *Must Know*

Johnny, Manual, Teresa, Joshua, Mary, Sam   33%

Tier 2: *Must Know, Should Know*

Brian, Gabriel, Rosa, Cathy   22%

Tier 1: *Must Know, Should Know, Could Know*

Lucas, Ray, Tanisha, Justin, Irina, Adrian,
Aaron, Annemarie   44%

Upon closer examination, Ms. Young determines that Sam now seems to need Tier 3 services and both Annemarie and Aaron are now performing at proficient levels. Ms. Young decides to refer Sam to the RtI team. Even though he is already receiving intervention, the results of summative assessment suggest that he may need a closer look. Additionally, Ms. Young advises the RtI Team that Aaron and Annemarie are performing at proficient levels and thus may no longer need intervention.

Practical Application: Reconfigure Your Class Triangle

Activity

Working with your own data, revise your student triangles. If you have not completed your first round of summative assessments, you can save this activity for a future date.

- In the first triangle, list the names of your students receiving instruction/intervention services in each tier
- In the second triangle, revise the list to reflect the results of your current summative assessment data.
- What conclusions can you draw based on the changes in your triangle?
- What actions will you take based on the analysis?
  - Should you alert your RtI team for any specific students?
  - Will your instruction change as a result of changes in your RtI triangle? How so?

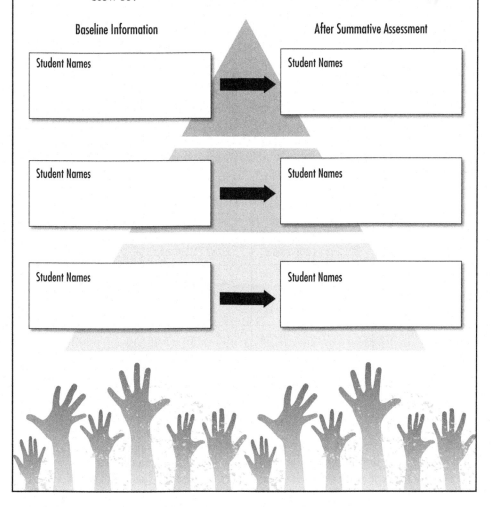

Baseline Information | After Summative Assessment

Student Names

Student Names

Student Names

Student Names

Student Names

Student Names

Use Summative Data to Reflect and Move Forward

In Chapter 4, we discussed reflecting on the previous year's assessments to make initial decisions about this year's instruction. Summative assessments provide the same opportunity, but this time, we reflect on our own instruction and student responses. Each summative assessment provides us the opportunity to ask ourselves some important questions:

- Did we teach the curriculum as designed?
- Did we attend to the *must know*, *should know*, and *could know* levels of standards acquisition to differentiate instruction?
- Did we adjust our instruction in response to pre-assessment and formative assessments?
- Did our instruction reflect the tasks and format of the external measures?
- Do our students demonstrate the same strengths and weaknesses they possessed at the beginning of the year?
  - Are students continuing to make progress in their areas of strength?
  - Has progress been made to turn weakness into strength?
- How will we improve our instruction moving forward based on the needs of the students?

The answers to these questions direct our plans for future instruction. Merely reviewing the data and moving forward without reflection or action guarantees that our results will not improve. The following example illustrates one teacher's response to summative assessment in Tier 1.

Mr. Garcia's Class—The table below depicts the average results of Mr. Garcia's 4th grade Language Arts class after the first trimester standards-based assessment. When Mr. Garcia examined the data from the previous year, he noted a class-wide weakness in grammar and comprehension. In response, Mr. Garcia provided more explicit instruction in those two strands. After the first trimester standards-based assessment, Mr. Garcia compared those results to the students' baseline data.

TABLE 7.1

Strand	Baseline: Last Year's performance	Current Performance	Growth
Vocabulary	4	4	No change
Comprehension	2	4	+2
Grammar	2	3	+1
Writing	3	2	-1
Standards concepts	4	4	No change

Although Mr. Garcia was pleased with the growth in comprehension and grammar, he noticed a drop in performance in the writing strand. Realizing that he has let writing slip in order to spend more time with grammar and comprehension, Mr. Garcia revised his instructional plans for the upcoming trimester to ensure that students would write about their reading. He also decided to make grammar part of the writing process to promote having students transfer grammar skills to their writing. Mr. Garcia made strategically targeted adjustments to bring up the writing scores while continuing to improve student performance in the remaining strands.

Reflection always requires action. Ideally, analysis of summative data serves to improve instruction and move our students forward. In the same way that we used the previous year's data to plan before the year began (see Chapter 4), Tier 1 summative assessment results help us plan for the next chapter, unit, semester, benchmark period, and finally the yearly state assessment. We have come full circle and begin the process anew.

Practical Application: Reflect and Look Forward

Activity

Use the following questions to analyze the results of your summative assessments and use that analysis to plan your future instruction.

- Analyze the results of your most recent summative assessments and compare them to previous summative assessment results.
- Use the analysis and comparison to answer the questions posed below.

Question	Reflection	Response Action
Did my students perform as expected?		
Did my instruction reflect the tasks and format of the external measures?		
Did I teach the curriculum as designed?		
Did I differentiate using must know, should know, and could know levels of standards acquisition?		
Did I use pre-assessment and formative assessment to tailor my lessons to student need?		
Did the patterns of strengths and weaknesses identified at the beginning of the year change or remain the same?		
Where do I need to adjust my instruction? How will that be accomplished?		

The Cycle of Assessment and Instruction *Cont. Improv.*

In Chapters 4–7, we have discussed the use of data at various points in the planning and instructional process. However, analysis of assessment results as well as our instructional response to the analysis does not end at the close of a chapter, unit, course of study, benchmark period, or even a year. Assessment and instruction generate a continuous cycle of data, information, and instructional response. Viewing this process as a recurring cycle and attending to that data emerge as integral parts of teaching Tier 1. The following graphic illustrates this cycle.

FIGURE 7.6

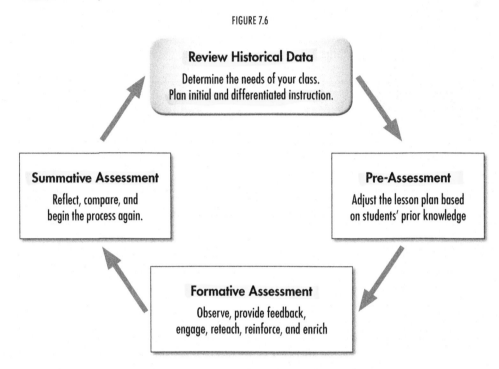

As we have emphasized throughout this book, Tier 1 is the foundation of an effective RtI system. In fact, the numbers of students requiring intervention services is a direct result of the design and implementation of the Tier 1 curriculum. In an effective RtI system, it is only through responsive data driven instruction, adjustment, and differentiation that we serve our proficient and advanced students while working to close the achievement gap for those who struggle.

Section 3
Considerations Beyond the Tier 1 Classroom

So far, we have emphasized that what Tier 1 teachers do in their classrooms is the critical variable in realizing the full potential of RtI; these educators are where the rubber meets the road to create a successful implementation. Yet Tier 1 teachers are not the whole story. They are part of a larger system, and there are factors in a successful RtI approach that lie beyond the control of the individual teacher. Decisions pertaining to infrastructure, policies, and overarching instructional goals typically emanate from school or district-wide leadership teams. Ideally, these decisions support and enable the work of the Tier 1 teacher. Awareness and understanding of these considerations strengthen teachers' ability to participate effectively in the development and implementation of an RtI system. For this reason, the final chapters focus on considerations that reach beyond the Tier 1 classroom. Chapter 8 examines some of the critical district and school-level decisions that impact Tier 1 instruction. The final chapter (9) features a checklist to inventory and guide the implementation of Tier 1 and offers real world examples of the planning and decision-making process. Together these chapters remain focused on the essential ingredients—curriculum, assessment, and instruction—and on the conversation that must take place between teachers and administrators to implement a strong Tier 1.

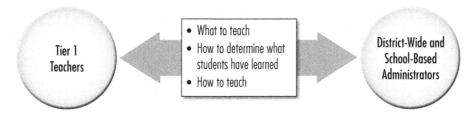

CHAPTER EIGHT

Tier 1 Considerations Beyond the Classroom Level

The foundation for a successful RtI plan is what happens in the Tier 1 classroom with a teacher who understands standards-based instruction, who employs effective instructional practices, and who uses data to inform instruction. Yet implementation of an effective RtI plan stretches beyond the individual teacher in the Tier 1 classroom. Leaders at the school and district level bear responsibility for an effective RtI plan, as well. Among the critical district-level factors that impact Tier 1 instruction are district administrators' awareness of the proportion of students in each tier for the purpose of curricular and organizational planning; recognition that there are changing cognitive demands on students as they progress from kindergarten to high school; resolution of issues surrounding cross-tier continuity; policies regarding core replacement; and the willingness to support multi-year professional development.

Implications of Tier Proportions

As we mentioned in the Introduction and examined at the classroom level in Chapter 4, knowing how closely a school fits the recommended 80–15–5 percent proportions impacts curricular decision-making. Let's look at some of the common tier configurations (Figure 8.1) and their implications at a school or district level. The proportions in each tier, derived from available data, help determine where curriculum decisions or adjustments are needed.

FIGURE 8.1

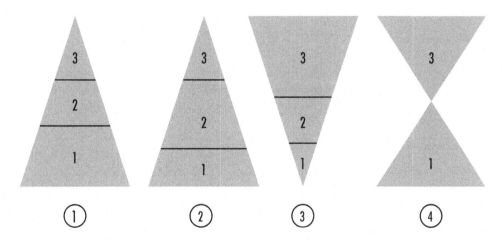

The following table (Table 8.1) illustrates school or district-wide considerations based on these common tier proportions.

TABLE 8.1

	1	2	3	4
Description	• A large percentage of students in Tier 1 suggests – High performing student population	• A proportionally large Tier 2 suggests – Gaps in the Tier 1 scope and sequence of content and skills – Overreliance on Tier 2 intervention rather than differentiation and explicit instruction in Tier 1	• Disproportionately small Tier 1, small Tier 2, and disproportionately large Tier 3 suggests – Significant gaps in standards-based performance	• No Tier 2, equal Tier 1 and Tier 3 suggests – Gaps in the Tier 1 scope and sequence of content and skills – Quick referral to Tier 3 intervention
Implication	• Consider ways to enrich Tier 1 curriculum for proficient and advanced students • Examine intervention practices for Tiers 2 and 3	• Examine Tier 1 scope and sequence for gaps • Improve Tier 1 instruction and include differentiation • Provide professional development for Tier 1 teachers regarding differentiating instruction	• Consider Tier 1 replacement core curriculum • Examine scope and sequence for instruction in Tier 1 • Examine benchmark and other assessment tools for relevance to state tests	• Develop Tier 2 interventions • Examine criteria for defining tiers • Examine scope and sequence for instruction in Tier 1 • Identify strategies for differentiating instruction in Tier 1 • Examine benchmark and other assessment tools for relevance to state tests

Administrative analysis of Tier 1 instruction helps ensure that schools consider the range of students in the class. Decisions growing out of this analysis improve the entire instructional system so that as many students as possible are successful in Tier 1.

The Changing Demands K–12

District and school-based leadership should also consider another factor that can influence an RtI plan—the seismic shift in demands on students as they progress from kindergarten through high school. This shift and its impact are particularly critical in the basic skills of reading/language arts and math given their foundational nature for success in all areas of academic pursuit. Decision-makers must be knowledgeable about the development of basic skills across the grades and understand how that influences the allocation of resources and organizational planning. Scheduling and staffing ratios, as well as the establishment of appropriate achievement expectations for different grade ranges, are all an outgrowth of this change in demands across the grades. Given the significance of this factor, let's take a closer look at this shift in reading and consider its impact.

In the primary grades, instruction is narrowly focused on building block skills. Instruction can be linear; assessment can target discrete skill acquisition. In secondary school, students face a much more complex task than in the primary grades. In the intermediate grades and beyond, where students are expected to read to learn, the content requires them to simultaneously use skills and concepts in an integrated way. Missing skills becomes like missing puzzle pieces and negatively impact comprehension and communication. For example (Figure 8.2), difficulty decoding a multi-syllabic word in science (e.g., pale gray) can have a ripple effect on vocabulary acquisition (e.g., medium gray) and reduce comprehension of text material (e.g., dark gray).

FIGURE 8.2

Building Blocks vs. Interlocking Puzzle Pieces

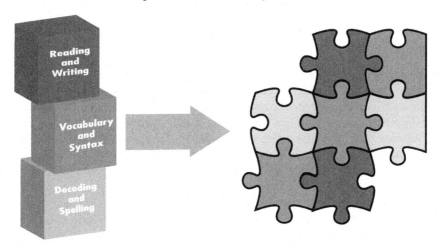

This factor also contributes to a shift in the purpose of our instruction, particularly for those students who struggle with the "must know" level of standards acquisition in content classes as well as the adopted English/Language Arts curriculum for Tier 1. Common sense and experience tell us that the purpose and potential of a multi-tiered model differ depending on the grade range of the students we are teaching.

The following table (Table 8.2) highlights this shift in purpose using literacy instruction as the example.

TABLE 8.2

	K–2	3–5	6–12
Purpose	Prevention	Minimize achievement gap through intensive literacy intervention	Maximize skill and content acquisition through intensive literacy intervention plus access
Instructional Focus	Target strategic skills	Comprehensive literacy instruction and intervention	Comprehensive literacy instruction concurrent with provisions to access content in social studies, science, and other core content areas

In the primary grades, when what students need to learn is relatively limited, preventing performance gaps is possible. Instruction can target strategic skills that can be measured precisely for the level of mastery. In the upper elementary grades, when students must use basic skills to learn other content, furnishing intensive intervention minimizes basic-skill achievement gaps. Once students hit the secondary grades, the instructional plan must provide alternative ways to access content in subjects for which the students' basic skills are insufficient to meet the demands. We refer to this approach for older struggling students as a dual solution—simultaneous attention to missing literacy skills concurrent with providing necessary accommodations. For example, electronic readers make it possible for students to access reading material at a higher level than they can read on their own. Using this type of technology, which makes it possible for students to listen to text they may not be able to read, allows students to access core content while simultaneously developing literacy proficiency. In this way, students can achieve the level of skill needed to access core content and concepts.

An Unintended Downside of Tier-Specific Programs: From the Student's Perspective

It is not unusual for districts or schools to develop an RtI model with materials and instructional practices specific for each tier of intervention. This practice of tier-specific programs can have an unintended downside for students as they make skill gains and attempt to transition to a less intensive tier. Often in tier-specific programs, skills are the same but the terminology and strategies differ, making the tasks appear "new" to the students. For example, one program may emphasize tackling multi-syllable words by chunking whereas another program emphasizes syllable division. The goal of both approaches is to decode unfamiliar words, but from the student's perspective, this looks like a new skill. This can also occur with more complex tasks such as identifying the main idea in text. When different teachers within or across grades or tiers present the same skill using different terminology, students on their own have to reconcile the similarities and differences, an inefficient approach, especially for the struggling learners. Rather than establishing a common approach across tiers to provide continuity from the student's perspective, tier-specific programs frequently make skill acquisition more complex due to the variety of ways the same skill can be taught. This point should not be confused, as was discussed in Chapter 2, with simply providing a double dose of the same intervention. The focus instead is on making cross-tier movement possible, an aspect of curricular decision-making that can facilitate (or hamper) students' success as they move from tier to tier. District and school leaders have the responsibility for keeping this factor in mind when selecting curricular materials and providers for professional development. Failure to keep this factor in mind can limit—often unintentionally—the ability of students to move to less intensive instructional settings.

The Threshold of Tier 1: When the Gap is Too Great—Core Replacement

Tier 1 creates the threshold of performance against which decisions to provide more instructional time and intensity are made. Simply put, the greater the distance from the core, the more severe the needs and the greater the intensity of the intervention (Figure 8.3). Regardless of the severity of need and the intensity of intervention, the ideal is to have all students participate in the core curriculum. At what point, however, is the gap too great?

FIGURE 8.3

Distance From Core

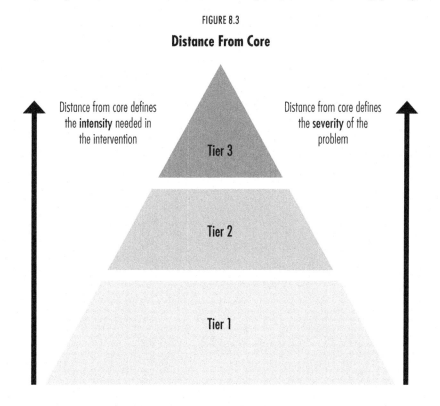

While some districts include all students in Tier 1 instruction, many districts and schools have decided to replace Tier 1 instruction for students requiring Tier 3 instruction, a practice that is more typical in grade 3 and higher. In these cases, the RtI team reviews student data and decides that the student is too far from grade level to benefit from core, that is standards-based grade level instruction. The RtI team makes a cost/benefit analysis in which participation in the core costs students more than it benefits them. The students' need for intervention outweighs the need for Tier 1 instruction in time, intensity, and content. This translates into Tier 1 replacement. While the logic of providing intensive intervention is easy to follow, this concept can give rise to some controversy if Tier 1 replacement denies access to Tier 1 concepts. When school or district administrators are aware of this potential issue, however, students do not have to be denied access to Tier 1 content. Tier 1 concepts are taught as part of the intervention block. The instruction of "must know" grade level concepts is delivered through differentiated instruction. By changing process and product and delivering instruction by alternative methods, students are able to fully participate. After students receiving intervention acquire skill levels that allow them to meet the demands of the core curriculum, they can return to Tier 1 instruction supplemented with Tier 2 services.

Supporting and Sustaining a Tier 1 Initiative

District and school leadership play a critical role in supporting the implementation of an effective RtI plan. Districts can achieve a more robust implementation of RtI if the leadership advocates the notion that Tier 1 teachers, including all subject-area teachers, are part of a larger network, all of which are focused on the common goal of having students master the skills and content of a standards-based curriculum. In addition to advocating the importance of a well-designed RtI initiative, district and school leadership are essential in assuring that logistics (such as scheduling) are consistent with optimal implementation. Finally, and perhaps most importantly, school district leadership can allocate resources to provide high quality professional development for district and staff. Quality Tier 1 instruction does not happen accidentally or overnight. It evolves slowly and with the assistance of internal or external experts. Professional development for RtI implementation can take many forms. It can be facilitation in planning and analysis, assessment, or instructional review. It can come in the form of training on instructional practice and response to data. As implementation evolves, it may take the form of on-site coaching. Whatever the nature or type of professional development, quality of Tier 1 instruction is not likely to happen without it.

CHAPTER NINE

Start Where You Are!

RtI is not a one-size-fits all initiative. Not all schools are in the same place and therefore each implementation follows a different path. RtI is, in fact, a way of thinking about instructional methods and content that will meet the needs of all students. In order to sustain tiered support, Tier 1 must be the foundation of our instructional program, not an add-on (Allain, 2008). In this book, we have demonstrated how to join a logically sequenced, standards based curriculum to data driven instructional response to construct a strong Tier 1 program. We will state again: *Tier 1 is the cornerstone of an RtI model. Without strong Tier 1 instruction, RtI will become a system of never-ending interventions rather than excellent first instruction.*

That said, any new initiative requires change or at the very least an analysis of what we are already doing. Through our work with districts and schools across the country, we have found that many of the components of RtI are already occurring in districts and schools. Even without the initiative, teachers and administrators understand that we must meet the needs of all students if we are to close the achievement gap and regain our status as an educational power. The secret to effective multi-tiered support is to analyze what is already being done, create an efficient structure that utilizes the RtI model, and identify those components that are lacking or insufficiently implemented.

The first step, then, is to analyze Tier 1 instruction and identify what you already have in place and what you need to put in place. The checklist on the following page cites the necessary components of Tier 1. Use this checklist to analyze the state of Tier 1 in your district or school. We have provided examples that illustrate how other districts or schools determined how and where to start to solidify Tier 1.

Tier 1 Checklist

TABLE 9.1

	Tier 1 Essentials	Fully Implemented	Partially Implemented	Not Implemented
Curriculum	Research and select evidence, and standards based curriculum.			
	Identify high value standards.			
	Develop a defined scope and sequence.			
	Define must know, should know, could know levels of standards acquisition.			
	Select curricular materials that contain culturally relevant selections at varied reading levels.			
	Ensure that the curriculum is taught as designed.			
Assessment	Develop and administer periodic standards based benchmark assessments.			
	Ensure that formative assessments are varied and ongoing.			
	Use common summative assessments for chapters, units, or courses of study.			
	Analyze data reporting and management for teacher accessibility and use.			
	Organize data compilation reports to be teacher friendly, efficiently organized, readily accessible, and timely.			
	Use pre-assessment, formative assessments, and summative assessments to gauge student progress.			
	Respond to data by adjusting instruction to students' assessed needs.			
	Define and articulate the threshold of Tier 1 for all Tier 1 teachers.			

Tier 1 Checklist (cont'd)

	Tier 1 Essentials	Fully Implemented	Partially Implemented	Not Implemented
Instruction	Teach the core curriculum as designed.			
	Identify student strengths and weaknesses before instruction.			
	Develop class RtI triangles.			
	Use the *must know*, *should know*, and *could know* levels of standards acquisition when planning and instructing students.			
	Use culturally relevant instruction.			
	Use accommodations and English learner strategies when appropriate.			
	Use frontloading (pre-teaching) when indicated by pre-assessment.			
	Deliver instruction in a combination of whole and small groups depending on need and activity.			
	Use a variety of engagement strategies.			
	Provide feedback to students in an instructive and timely manner.			
	Use gradual release of responsibility, taking into account student need.			
	Use re-teaching, reinforcement, and enrichment on a regular basis as indicated by data.			
	Define differentiated instruction and apply based on data.			

District and School Examples

Example 1:
District Profile: Moderate Size, Rural District; Large EL Population

The district in Example 1 had begun to implement an RtI system in its schools. As part of the planning, the district analyzed what parts of such a system were already in place and which needed restructuring. Additionally, the district team analyzed the effects of their Tier 1 instruction. The curriculum portion of its checklist looked as follows:

TABLE 9.2

Curriculum	Fully Implemented	Partially Implemented	Not Implemented
Research and select evidence, and standards based curriculum.	X		
Identify high value standards.		X	
Develop a defined scope and sequence.		X	
Define must know, should know, could know levels of standards acquisition.		X	
Select curricular materials that contain culturally relevant selections at varied reading levels.		X	
Ensure that the curriculum is taught as designed.		X	

As the district team probed the information in the checklist, they found that:

- The scope of the curriculum was standards based but the sequence varied from class to class.
- High value standards had not been identified across the district.
- Curricular tasks did not always match external measures.
- Differentiated instruction was implemented but was not based on difficulties students were having in Tier 1.
- Materials selection varied from teacher to teacher and instruction was not always culturally relevant.
- Fidelity to instruction could not be readily determined due to lack of continuity of instruction.

As a result of the district team's analysis and input from site principals, the team decided to take these steps first:

- Research and select a core curriculum beginning in K-2 that adhered to research-based literacy instruction with a strong, explicit phonemic awareness and phonics component.

- Identify high value standards and use those to define the scope and sequence of instruction.
- Ensure that the materials selected contain culturally relevant selections and activities.

Example 2:
District Profile: Large Suburban, Moderate Socioeconomic and EL Population

This district had already begun to implement an RtI system through pilots at selected schools at the elementary, middle, and high school levels. When administrators expanded the implementation to the entire district and analyzed current practices, some gaps became apparent. Careful analysis indicated that:

- Benchmarks had been developed for Reading/Language Arts and math but only math had been fully implemented.
- Common summative assessments were used in some buildings but not others; therefore using summative assessments to inform instruction was difficult in some buildings.
- Data analysis was occurring in department or grade level teams but not in a systematic way partially due to data accessibility.
- A threshold for Tier 1 had not been identified.

TABLE 9.3

Assessment	Fully Implemented	Partially Implemented	Not Implemented
Develop and administer periodic standards based benchmark assessments.		X	
Ensure that formative assessments are varied and ongoing.	X		
Use common summative assessments for chapters, units, or courses of study.		X	
Analyze data reporting and management for teacher accessibility and use.		X	
Organize data compilation reports to be teacher friendly, efficiently organized, readily accessible, and timely.			X
Use pre-assessment, formative assessments, and summative assessments to gauge student progress.		X	
Respond to data by adjusting instruction to students, assessed needs.	X		
Define and articulate the threshold of Tier 1 for all Tier 1 teachers.			X

In response to this analysis, the district moved forward on the following items.

- Implement standards based benchmarks across the district. This would also solidify the sequence of instruction in Tier 1.
- Encourage buildings to develop common summative assessments in all content areas to assist in instructional response.
- Purchase a data system that would enable teachers to easily access student data for data meetings, reports, and parent meetings.
- Define the threshold of Tier 1:
  - Implement reading screens at K–2 and Grades 3–12 to be given three times per year across the district.
  - Use cut points on the state test, benchmarks, and reading screens to identify students who may need intervention.
  - Provide professional development for teachers to identify students in need of intervention between benchmark periods.

Example 3:
School Profile: Large Urban Secondary School; Low Socioeconomic Level

This large urban school had been making steady progress with its Tier 1 instruction but wanted to increase the rate of student achievement. After analyzing Tier 1 data, administrators found that most of the instructional components were in place but realized that student performance on formative and summative assessment data did not generalize to the district benchmark assessments or the state assessments.

TABLE 9.4

Instruction	Fully Implemented	Partially Implemented	Not Implemented
Teach the core curriculum as designed.	X		
Curricular tasks match external measures.		X	
Identify student strengths and weaknesses before instruction.	X		
Develop class RtI triangles.	X		
Use the must know, should know, could know levels of standards acquisition when planning and instructing students.	X		
Use culturally relevant instruction.	X		

TABLE 9.4 (CONT'D)

Instruction	Fully Implemented	Partially Implemented	Not Implemented
Use accommodations and English learner strategies when appropriate.	X		
Use frontloading (pre-teaching) when indicated by pre-assessment.	X		
Deliver instruction in a combination of whole and small groups depending on need and activity.	X		
Use a variety of engagement strategies.	X		
Provide feedback to students in an instructive and timely manner.	X		
Use gradual release of responsibility, taking into account student need.	X		
Use re-teaching, reinforcement, and enrichment on a regular basis as indicated by data.	X		
Define differentiated instruction and apply as indicated by data.	X		

Further investigation revealed that the type, format, and vocabulary of the external measures (benchmark and state assessments) were not reflected in the ongoing Tier 1 assignments and assessments. In order to remedy that, the staff at this school analyzed the external measures and took the following steps:

- Identified high frequency academic vocabulary that was used on external measures.
  - Selected an academic vocabulary word of the week that was taught and reinforced by the entire staff.
- Identified the format, syntax, and structure of the questions on the external measures and included them in class assignments and assessments.
- Consciously increased academic vocabulary during instruction.
- Taught question interpretation strategies in all subject areas.

Example 4:
School Profile: Mid-Size Suburban K–8

The school in Example 4 was just beginning to implement an RtI system. As part of the development of its system, leadership analyzed the core instruction as it related to the parameters of Tier 1. Most all components were in place but when working with staff, school leaders realized that they had been differentiating for all students for so long that they were unclear about what should be expected if students were to perform at proficient levels in class and on external measures.

TABLE 9.5

Curriculum	Fully Implemented	Partially Implemented	Not Implemented
Research and select evidence, and standards based curriculum.	X		
Identify high value standards.	X		
Develop a defined scope and sequence.	X		
Define *must know, should know, could know* levels of standards acquisition.			X
Select curricular materials containing culturally relevant selections at varied reading levels.	X		
Ensure that the curriculum is taught as designed.	X		

As a result of that epiphany, the staff worked with a consultant and their curricular materials to determine the *must know*, *should know*, and *could know* levels of standards acquisition for the high value standards. Working through this process helped not only to identify the level of what it means to be proficient but also the type of differentiated instruction that would be necessary for students in the *could know* range (advanced, gifted) and the *must know* (students already receiving intervention) range of performance. The adoption of an RtI system helped the staff to define the parameters and focus on Tier 1 instruction.

Example 5:
School Profile: Large Urban Elementary School, Low Socioeconomic Level

When analyzing Tier 1, the staff at this school found that their curricular and assessment components were in place and used as designed. However, when they analyzed the instructional component, the staff found that although their instruction was good, some important components of instruction were not fully implemented.

- Teachers were generally but not specifically aware of the performance levels of the students in their classes.
- Teachers could not identify the strengths and weaknesses of their students.

- Primary method of delivery was whole group with a designated time for small group differentiation that was not always informed by data.
- Engagement strategies were varied and not consistently used across campus.

TABLE 9.6

Instruction	Fully Implemented	Partially Implemented	Not Implemented
Teachers identify student strengths and weaknesses before instruction.	X		
Teachers have developed their own class pyramids.		X	
Teachers use the must know, should know, could know levels of standards acquisition when planning and instructing students.	X		
Culturally relevant instruction is in place.	X		
Teachers use accommodations and English learner strategies when appropriate.	X		
Frontloading (pre-teaching) is used when indicated by pre-assessment.	X		
Instruction is delivered in a combination of whole and small groups depending on need and activity.		X	
A variety of engagement strategies are used.		X	
Feedback is provided to students in an instructive and timely manner.	X		
Teachers employ the strategy of gradual release of responsibility, taking into account students needs.	X		
Re-teaching, reinforcement, and enrichment occur on a regular basis as indicated by data.	X		
Differentiated instruction is defined and applied as indicated by data.		X	

After identifying areas of need, the staff at this school embarked on a year-long professional development project to bring their instruction to the fully implemented level.

- All teachers created class pyramids based on the results of the state and periodic benchmark assessments and identified student achievement goals.

- Data from benchmark assessments were used to identify patterns of strengths and weaknesses in each class so that teachers could design focus areas for their classes.

- Formative and summative assessments were analyzed to determine the focus of small group instruction during differentiation time.

- High leverage engagement strategies were identified that could be used across content and grade levels. The first four identified strategies are listed below.

  - Purposeful choral repetition and response when appropriate
  - Partner work and process time
  - Randomization for calling on students to answer questions
  - Moving around the classroom

Although both assessment and anecdotal data were monitored throughout the year, the staff was eager to see the results of the state assessment. The results of the current and previous year were then analyzed to see if the instructional changes had affected the results. The results of both years' assessments are illustrated below. The staff realized that they had more work to do but were pleased with initial student growth.

TABLE 9.7

Grade	Proficient and Advanced 2009	Proficient and Advanced 2010
2	42%	64%
3	29%	34%
4	41%	54%
5	32%	45%

Example 6:
School Profile: Mid Size Suburban Elementary School; Large EL Population

Multi-tiered instruction and intervention were well developed in this elementary school. All students were assessed on a regular basis and skill groups were formed to address student needs. All students attended small group intervention at a specific time of the day during which skills were taught and progress was monitored. Movement of students, student engagement, and skill instruction were exceptionally organized, analyzed, and effective. However, upon examination it was discovered that the majority of the students in this school still required intervention. That analysis caused the site intervention team to further analyze their Tier 1 instruction based on the question, "How can we ensure that more students are proficient in Tier 1 and reduce the need for intervention?"

TABLE 9.8

Curriculum	Fully Implemented	Partially Implemented	Not Implemented
Research and select evidence, and standards based curriculum.		X	
Identify high value standards.	X		
Develop a defined scope and sequence.		X	
Define *must know, should know, could know* levels of standards acquisition.	X		
Select curricular materials that contain culturally relevant selections at varied reading levels.	X		
Ensure that the curriculum is taught as designed.			X

As a result of the analysis, the team realized that all teachers were not covering the skills and concepts equally. As a consequence, students may have been referred to intervention for skills not taught, rather than skills not learned. Moreover, activities in Tier 1 skill groups were more busy work than enrichment. Finally, the team realized that the current curriculum did not cover academic vocabulary to the extent necessary and that the reading and writing portion of the curriculum were not correlated. Based on this analysis, the team decided to do the following;

- Dedicate meeting time to Tier 1 analysis in order to:
  - Analyze the skills taught in intervention against the skills covered in Tier 1 to see if a gap existed in first instruction.
  - Ensure that all teachers taught all components of the Tier 1 curriculum with required emphasis.
  - Correlate the reading and writing portions of the curriculum so that students write about their reading.
  - Identify and enrich the academic vocabulary portion of their curriculum.
  - Develop enrichment and extension activities for Tier 1 groups during skills groups.

Every district and school is at a different point in the development of a fully functional RtI system. The examples listed above demonstrate that it is critical to start where you are. Careful analysis may reveal that some Tier 1 components are in place but need restructuring; other elements may be conspicuously absent, and still others may be right on target. Whatever the case, working through the details of good first instruction is the foundation of RtI.

REFERENCES

Allain, J. (2008). *Logistics of Literacy Intervention: An RtI Planning Guide for Elementary Schools.* Longmont, CO: Sopris West Educational Services.

Batsche, G., Elliott, J., Graden, J. L., Grimes, J., Kovaleski, J.G, Prasse, D., Reschly, D. J., Schrag, J., & Tilly III, D.W. (2006). *Response to Intervention: Policy Considerations and Implementations.* Alexandria, VA. National Association of State Directors of Special Education.

Buffum, A., Mattos, M. & Chris Weber. (2009) *Pyramid Response to Intervention: RTI, Professional Learning Communities and How to Respond When Kids Don't Learn.* Bloomington, IN: Solution Tree Press.

Chall, J. S. (1983). *Stages of Reading Development.* New York: McGraw–Hill Book Company.

Christenson, S. L., & Ysseldyke, J. E. (1989). Assessing student performance: An important change is needed. *The Journal of School Psychology, 27.* 409–425.

City, E.A., Elmore, R. F., Fiarman, S. E., & Lee Teitel. (2010) *Instructional Rounds in Education: A Network Approach to Improving Speaking and Learning.* Cambridge, MA: Harvard Education Press.

Degrees of Reading Power: Users Manual: Test Description, Score Interpretation and Technical Information. Touchstone Applied Science Associates (TASA), NY

Dutro, S. & Moran, C. (2002). *Rethinking English Language Instruction: An Architectural Approach.* Chapter prepared for English Learners: Reaching the Highest Level of English Literacy, Gilbert Garcia, Editor, International Reading Association

Fischer, D. & Frey, N. (2003) Writing instruction for struggling adolescent readers: A gradual release model. *Journal of Adolescent and Adult Literacy, 46, 396–407.*

Gettinger, M. & Seibert, J. K. (2002). Best practices in increasing academic learning time. In Thomas, A., & Grimes, J. (Eds.), *Best practices in school psychology, IV* (pp. 773–787). Bethesda, MD: The National Association of School Psychologists.

Gickling, E. E., & Armstrong, D. L. (1978). Levels of instructional difficulty as related to on-task behavior, task completion, and comprehension. *Journal of Learning Disabilities.* 11, 559–566.

Gickling, E. & Thompson, V. (1985). A personal view of curriculum-based assessment. *Exceptional Children*, 52, 205–218.

Greene, J.F. (1998). Another Chance. *American Educator*, Spring-Summer.

Gusky, T. R. (2010) Mastery Learning: The core elements of mastery learning provide the foundation for other innovative models, including Response to Intervention. *Educational Leadership*, 68(2), 53–57

Guthrie, J. T., & Wigfield, A. (2000). Engagement and motivation in reading. In M. L. Kamil, P. B. Mosenthal, P. D. Pearson, & R. Barr (Eds.), *Handbook of reading research* (Vol. 3, pp. 403–420). Mahwah, NJ: Erlbaum.

Heritage, Margaret. (2010) *Formative Assessment and Next-Generation Assessment Systems: Are We Losing an Opportunity*. Paper prepared for Council of Chief State School Officers, Washington, DC (retrieved 11-9-10) www.edweek.org/ew/articles/2010/11/10/12assess.h30.html?tkn=TNTFgrGAAaTla7uAp2cnfPpuQpnZqTq%2BoFyD&cmp=clp-edweek

Kong, A, & Pearson, P.D. (2003) The road to participation: The construction of a literacy practice in a learning community of linguistically diverse learners. *Research in the Teaching of English, 38, 85–124*

Kucik, S. *The Triangle is the Goal; What is Your Reality?*, Presentation given at Clark County Schools, Las Vegas, Nevada, 2009

Lembke, E. retrieved from National Center on Response to Intervention website, video transcript, retrieved from Internet 8-13-10

Lemov, D. (2010) *Teach Like a Champion*, San Francisco, CA: Jossey-Bass.

Lloyd, S. L. (2004) Using comprehension strategies as a springboard for student talk. *Journal of Adolescent and Adult Literacy, 48, 114–124.*

Marzano, R. (2003) What works in schools: Translating research into action. Alexandria, VA: Association for Supervision and Curriculum Development.

Marzano, R.J. & Kendall, John S. (2008) *Designing & Assessing Educational Objectives: Applying the New Taxonomy.* Thousand Oaks, CA: Corwin Press.

Paribakht, T., & Wesche, M. (1997). Vocabulary enhancement activities and reading for meaning in second language vocabulary acquisition. In J. Coady & T. Huckin (Eds.), *Second language vocabulary acquisition: A rationale for pedagogy* (pp. 174–200). Cambridge, England: Cambridge University Press.

Pearson, P.D. & Gallagher, M.C. (1983). The instruction of reading comprehension. *Contemporary Educational Psychology*, 8, 317–344.

Rosenfield, Sylvia A. (1987). *Instructional Consultation*, Hillsdale, New Jersey: Lawrence Erlbaum Associates.

Schmoker, Mike. (2010). When Pedagogic Fads Trump Priorities. *Education Week*, September 27, 2010.

Pogrow, S. (1998). Reforming the wannabe reformers: why education reforms almost always end up making things worse, *Phi Delta Kappan.*

Vygotsky, L. S. (1962). *Thought and Language.* Cambridge: MIT Press.

CPSIA information can be obtained at www.ICGtesting.com
Printed in the USA
BVOW04s0212150916

462131BV00005B/62/P

9 780983 397151